Robert William Ashburner

Shorthorn experiences

Written at the request of a few breeders

Robert William Ashburner

Shorthorn experiences
Written at the request of a few breeders

ISBN/EAN: 9783337147136

Printed in Europe, USA, Canada, Australia, Japan

Cover: Foto ©Andreas Hilbeck / pixelio.de

More available books at **www.hansebooks.com**

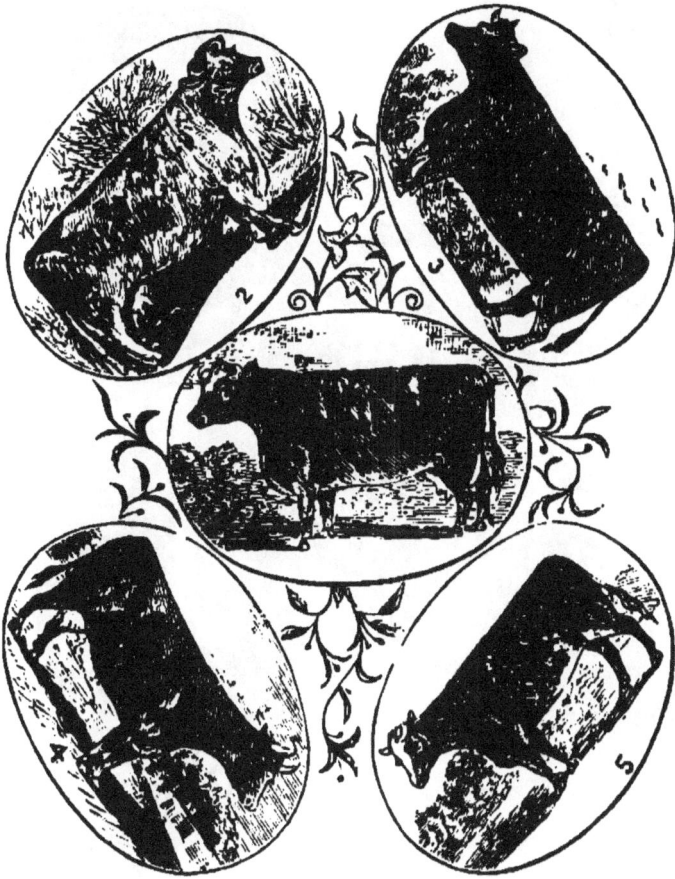

See Page 201.

PRUDENCE

PERSEVERANCE

EXPERIENCE

PREJUDICE

FASHION

See Page 200.

SHORTHORN

EXPERIENCES,

(WRITTEN AT THE REQUEST OF A FEW BREEDERS,)

BY

WILLIAM ASHBURNER,

The Manor House, Moreton, Warwick.

WARWICK:

HENRY T. COOKE & SON, HIGH STREET,

LONDON: SIMPKIN, MARSHALL & Co.

CONTENTS.

ERRATA.

PAGE.

35—Lines 7 and 19, Samartine, *read* Lamartine.

57—Line 3, confirmed, *read* compared.

71—Line 2, unite, *read* write.

71—Line 6, having, *read* leaving.

113—Line 11, it is in making, *read* but in making.

122—Line 3, was, *read* were.

139—Lines 18 and 21, Barnyeat, *read* Burnyeat.

149—Line 13, he was not then young in years, and not far advanced in years of experience in shorthorn breeding, *read* although advanced in years he was but young in the experience of shorthorn breeding.

166—Line 18, there, *read* where.

176—Line 12, not pretty enough for the dairy, *read* and not even that for the dairy.

182—Line 4, provoking, *read* creating.

INTRODUCTION.

THE Author of this small work has frequently been requested by several friends, and shorthorn breeders, to write a short account upon his experience in shorthorns, as well as giving a few illustrations, respecting the doings of breeders of the past. He has at last, yet, very reluctantly, taken up his pen, to commence to write upon this important question, it has taken him months, he may say more, even years, to make up his mind to appear in print; having acceded to their wishes, he trusts that they will deal leniently with him, in not criticising his remarks too severely, but pass over any errors he may unavoidably make, with a gentle reproof; but having had considerable experience in breeding, he dare not hope to be altogether passed by un-criticized, neither can he boast of any information that he can give to the experienced, will be worthy of notice, but perhaps, to the inexperienced,

> " Or to one, that is not a shorthorn breeder born,
>
> Or to one, that has not by shorthorns had his pocket
> threadbare worn,"

it may be of interest, to be guided a little by the writer, who has passed through a number of years in the rising and falling of the prices of shorthorns, as well as the changes that have taken place in the rising and falling of their popularity, in addition to being a breeder for a quarter of a century.

It is not an easy matter for an amateur in writing to explain minutely his experience in life, even if that experience be principally upon short-horns. The writer looks upon experience as a great master, a master of arts, full of years, and honour, one, that is capable of teaching others as he has been taught many valuable lessons to be remembered through life; and in writing this small volume for publication, he shall dwell principally upon Experience, and his four pupils, viz. Prudence, Perseverance, Fashion, and Prejudice ; the two former are far advanced in their scholarship, and agreeable companions, the two latter, quite the reverse, slow to learn, and unsociable when in companionship, but apart from Prejudice, the writer has found by experience that Fashion, united with Prudence and Perseverance, can be both agreeable and profitable. To give satisfactory pooof of this, he shall endeavour to show, how the union of the three pupils of experience, assisted him, in becoming not only a fashionable, but practical, and profitable shorthorn breeder ; had they been divided, or prejudice admitted, it would have been a complete failure. To arrive at this clearly, he will appear as a scholar, commencing with the alphabet on shorthorn breed-

ing, and undergo three examinations—the preliminary, intermediate, and final—which he shall
explain in three different chapters, by three successful sales that took place as he advanced by
experience as a breeder.

The writer has fully made up his mind, not to
allow prejudice to interfere with his description of
either any breed of cattle, or breeder. Although he
is an admirer of Bates' blood, it shall not be puff'd
up beyond its merits in the book which he has
decided to write in two parts, the first to contain
experience from breeders of the past, with remarks
by the Author. The second part, will give a brief
explanation of his experience in life, from childhood,
to boyhood, and from boyhood, to manhood, to
extend over a period of forty years, and by the
experience gained, would advise the young or inexperienced breeder—

   " To breed the beast, to fill the pail ;
    To breed the beast, to graze hill or dale ;
    To breed the beast, that will quick mature ;
    To breed the beast, that will all piercing winds endure."

SHORTHORN EXPERIENCES.

CHAPTER I.

HOW MESSRS. COLLINGS BRED THEIR SHORTHORNS, AFTERWARDS CALLED BATES' TRIBES.

The writer thinks it more prudent to relate briefly the experiences of one or two eminent breeders before that of his own, which have taught him many valuable lessons; although they have passed away from us, their experience is still with us, recorded in many a shorthorn history, and he may add almost invaluable to the inexperienced. But I imagine the experienced will probably say, what is the good of repeating the old story over and over again; tell us something new, and interesting, and not relate the old dried material of almost a century ago. If this be his opinion, the writer

surely differs from him.   He has made up his mind
to give his readers fully two chapters of the experiences of others, in the early part of the present
century, who paid even a higher price for it than we
at the present time.

It is now just over one hundred years, since
Mr. Charles Collings purchased at Stanwick Park,
his first Duchess cow, for the sum of £13.   The
same period of years have also elapsed, since he had
the pleasure of giving his brother Robert and Mr.
Waistell his advice, as to the purchase of a little
bull, that he had seen grazing in a field when taking
a walk a few days previous, which he thought might
be bought cheap, and answer their purpose until a
large calf of their own breeding was of sufficient
age.   Not thinking for one moment that the animal
was beyond ordinary merit, but simply that he
might do for the time required, at last the bull was
purchased for the sum of 8 guineas, certainly not a
very extravagant price for a beast at 7 years of age,
which won the first prize at Durham Agricultural
Show the same year, for the best aged shorthorn
bull, and that bull was named " Hubback (319.")
Not even the shrewdest of shorthorn breeders could
have discerned at so early a date, the astounding
results the union of these two animals would at a
future day bring forth ; it takes time and experience,
to carry out practically the breeder's part.   The

Duchess cow, being a daughter of James Brown's Red Bull (97), was put to Hubback, the produce of their union being a heifer, and that heifer in due time mated with Favourite (252), which again resulted in a female, when of sufficient age, was put to Daisy Bull (186) a son of Favourite (252) and the produce proved to be "Old Duchess," the dam of Ketton (709) one of the most wonderful bulls in his day, he was also a son of Favourite (252). Old Duchess, was the dam of an own sister to Ketton and that sister was the dam of "Young Duchess," by Comet (155), also a son of Favourite (252) purchased by Mr. Bates for 183gs. in Mr. Charles Collings' sale in 1810, and her sire Comet, realizing 1000gs. the same day to four breeders jointly, viz. Wetherell, Trotter, Wright, and Charge. "Young Duchess," is the ancestress of all Duchesses, and Grand Duchesses, now in existence, either in England, or any other part of the world. Thus far, we see the increase in value, and numbers of the Duchess family in the space of 16 years, between Mr. C. Collings purchasing for £13, and selling at £192, having previously sold the dam of Ketton for 100gs. to Mr. Bates.

As I am advancing rather too quickly with my history, kindly allow me to return again to the days—

"When Brothers' Collings as breeders made their name,
Through them alone, " Hubback," gained his fame."

Mr. Robert Collings, and Mr. Waistell, had Hubback
only a very short period, before asking their former
adviser if he knew of a customer for the animal.
Mr. Charles immediately replied, " I will take him
at the price you gave for him." Shortly after he
was sold, Mr. Waistell noticing the merits of the
bull as a quick thriver, to be rather extraordinary,
wished to send some of his cows to him, but Charles
Collings refused his request, unless he paid five
guineas per cow.   This exorbitant demand, after
receiving only four guineas for half of the beast,
taught Mr. Waistell that Mr. Charles Collings' advice
was worth remembering.   This same Mr. Waistell
was the first person to turn Mr. Bates' attention to
highly bred cattle, a lesson dearly bought is often
well remembered, as he evidently impressed upon
Mr. Bates the value of Hubback's blood. Apparently
from what we read, the latter would have tired the
most patient listener by sounding the praise of
Hubback ; as tracing direct to Hubback, was Mr.
Bates's motto to get the best of blood.   But what
became of Hubback ? some might inquire.   Why,
he was sold at 10 years of age for 30gs., and after
that time made a wonderful impression as a sire
whenever he was used, even upon ordinary dairy
stock.   He was only a small bull, and we are
informed that is why Mr. Charles Collings sold
him, because purchasers of his animals were fond
of size.   No doubt it is a great mistake, and one

made almost daily in the nineteenth century. A
massive, well-proportioned sire, is the one to leave
his mark behind him; beware of long legs, long
heads, and thin thighs. The writer remembers
about 30 years ago, two neighbouring farmers who
vied each other in their bulls. One was fond of a
good animal upon short legs, the other of one upon
a large bony scale to make some weight in the end
as he expressed himself. At last the two bulls
ended their days by being made into cash, the
small one in exchange for £40, to a home butcher,
but the large frame had to be sent to a manufac-
turing town, at some distance, before he could be
got rid of, after some difficulty the owner obtained
a bid of £35 and had to accept it with many thanks.
Well might Messrs. Collings, Waistell, and Bates
attach great importance to the blood of Hubback,
for the influence he had for good on their stock,
compared with what other sires had done. We
never hear of any miraculous results from the service
of the large bull preferred before him by Messrs.
Waistell and Collings, but we have it impressed
upon us over and over again, about the value
attached to the relationship of the little bull who
once grazed the lanes of Haughton, and ran by the
side of the blacksmith's cow—

> " But at last he stood as a noble sire,
>   Both for his friends and foes to admire."

But when we read of his dam being bred by Mr.

B

Stephenson of Ketton before Mr. Charles Collings went there to reside, need we wonder that this remarkable animal was so highly appreciated, as the Stephensons continued to cling to this blood, through the Princess tribe, for at least a century, and the same family ranks one of the first in fashion unto this day. Mr. Robert Collings too, was a great admirer of the descendants of the little fellow, in founding the Red Rose family, which told their own tale at his sale in 1818, by making the highest prices; for instance Lancaster (360), at 4 years old 621gs., and two females of the same line of blood realizing 300, and 331gs., respectively. This family, known as the Cambridge Roses in Mr. Bates' day, and at the present time as the "Thorndale Roses," here we have three noted families, tracing to Hubback, through the Duchesses, Red Roses, and Princesses, as well as the Daisies, which descend through Major (398) Windsor (698) Punch (531) and lastly Hubback. This family was then in high repute, but through intermingling with too many varieties of blood, although once so famous before the public, has gradually fallen away to be surpassed by many other families. The "Charmers," which descend through Sylph by Sir Walter (2627) Hotspur (1117) Coxcomb (928) Midas (435) Rachel by Comet (115) Russells by R. Collings' son of Favourite (252) repeated a second time by the same son of that most popular sire of his day, lastly

Hubback, which is the foundation of this most evenly bred tribe, it has passed through the hands of men of both judgment and influence in the short-horn circle. Its popularity as a tribe has ebbed a little, but will return gradually, if the personal appearance and the breeding is kept up to its present standard. As a pedigree it reads well, and bears criticism, as animals, they are generally true made, and robust, without coarseness. The Daisies having same foundation, and full of Collings' best blood, will not at present, bear out the examination so closely, but no doubt with perseverance, and pru-dence by their present owners, they will attain the celebrity they held in the days of Messrs. Collings, when Daisy Bull (186) was thought of sufficient merit to unite with the dam of Duchess of 1804. I must not omit the descendants of Mr. Robert Collings " Wildair," as tracing direct to Hubback, through a double cross of Favourite (252) and Ben (70) who also claims his ancestry to the son of the famed blacksmith's cow. The Wildairs, are now distinguished by the name of the " Flowers," having passed through Mr. Torr's hands for generations, contain a considerable dash of Warlaby blood, and are still a fine tribe of cattle, which were distributed to different breeders at the dispersion of the Aylesby herd, after Mr. Torr's death, when the Flowers were in full bloom, and made an average of £576 for 25 animals.

The only other branch descended from Wildair
by Favourite, are named Fama's or Fatima's and
are in the possession of the Duke of Manchester.
They are now crossed with Bates' bulls, and
admitted to be highly descended since the days of
Brothers Collings, without being bound by prejudice
to the purity of one line of blood, still this pedigree
·can claim 17 generations without a single stain in
their breeding.

But we must be awake and not caught slumber-
ing our time away, it requires thought, and careful
watching, to surpass what our ancestors did before
us, but experience alone, will teach us where to be
certain they erred in judgment; they had reasons
we know not of, for using certain males, and buying
animals of certain families, in many instances it
was an experiment for our benefit, which makes me
feel loath to condemn the judgment of any breeders
of shorthorns, who spent the best part of their lives
almost a century back in the improvement of the
breed of cattle; but many thanks are due to such
eminent men as Messrs. Mason, Wetherell, Trotter,
Wright, Charge, Whittaker, Maynard, and many
others, including John Hunter, the breeder of Hubback, who had even then a type of cattle difficult to
surpass.   It behoves us to breed with judgment and
not to let our animals deteriorate, to be surpassed
by other nations, in being led away by supporting

weeds, in place of robust plants, because they are
more fashionable ; adhere to the sorts that are good,
not only in pedigree, but good in themselves, and
cleave to the class of animals well tried for generations, and not because they are now simply prize
winners, it is rarely we hear of their progeny being
either numerous or prosperous.

CHAPTER II.

HOW MR. BATES BRED THE DUCHESSES AND THE RESULT.

In the last chapter we left Mr. Bates as a purchaser at Mr. C. Collings sale in 1810, of young Duchess for 183gs., an amateur in shorthorns might wonder who purchased the other animals descended from the "Stanwick Duchess," there were none for sale, a sad tale to relate, but it is too true to be forgotten, an experienced owner of cattle like Mr. C. Collings to breed from the grand cow as we have her described in Bell's history, and to have but one female descendant, and one male, named Duke (226), in the space of 16 years, but need we wonder at it, as the blood of Hubback, and Favourite, are repeated in every cross from the foundation, nor can any constitution stand it, it is impossible to go so far against nature, it appears to the writer that some of our early breeders took a delight to breeding in, and in, as much as possible, through their pet sires, throwing away constitution, by prejudice, and reaping their reward by being taught a lesson of experience, either by lack of constitution, or being unprolific. Mr. Bates undoubtedly was a shrewd man of business, and a good judge of cattle, keen to detect the errors in the judgment of others, but while smiling at them, did he always detect the errors in himself, I

am afraid not, experience taught him many a bitter
lesson, because prejudice fought hard against him,
which is most ruinous to shorthorn breeding, but
however resistent, sooner or later, will have to give
way to its master experience. I have said Mr. Bates
was a shrewd man, but I will say more, I believe he
was a man most honourable in all his transactions,
and particular in having good sires in his herd, which
undoubtedly is one of the most essential points in
shorthorn breeding. Allow me now to point out how
Mr. Bates began to breed, with his in bred "Duchess,"
having already two direct crosses of Favourite, and
two indirect, he puts her to Ketton 1st (709), also a
son of Favourite, from old Duchess, by Daisy Bull,
being a son of Favourite, and his grand-dam by
Favourite, followed by Hubback, the result of the
union is Duchess 2nd ; three years after she produces
Duchess 3rd, by the same sire, and in the two
following years, she produces Duchess 4th, and 5th,
by Ketton 2nd, (710), a son of Ketton 1st, but
from a different family, and lastly, she produces
Cleveland, by Ketton 3rd (349), he is by Ketton
2nd, from Duchess 3rd, by Ketton 1st, Duchess 2nd,
a daughter of Ketton 1st, is put to Ketton 2nd, and
then to Ketton 3rd, a son of Duchess 3rd, own sister
to Duchess 2nd, she is mated with Marske (418), a
bull with three successive crosses of Favourite,
followed by Punch, and Hubback, Duchess 3rd, and
4th, are also put to Marske, Duchess 3rd next

produces two calves to Duke (226), own brother to
Duchess 1st, Duchess 5th, by Ketton 2nd, from
Duchess 1st, has her first calf to " His Grace " (311),
a son of Ketton 2nd, from Duchess 2nd, by Ketton
1st, Duchess 10th, is by Cleveland (146), a son of
Ketton 3rd, and Duchess 1st, as far as I can trace,
to the year 1821, when Duchess 10th was calved.
Mr. Bates had then bred 9 Duchesses, and 8 Dukes,
from Duchess 1st, by Comet in the space of a little
over 10 years, all the 17 calves are bred in, and in, to
the highest degree, no change of blood is admitted,
except a little in Ketton 2nd, and Marske, and
that only in very small proportions, it is not until
1825 that he again admits any fresh blood to
his Duchess's and that is by the use of 2nd Hubback
(1423), a son of the Earl, an in-bred Duke, 2nd
Hubbacks dam, is Mr. Hustler's Red Rose, by
Yarborough (705), a son of Cupid, whose dam was
by Favourite, gr. d. by Hubback, the 3rd cross in 2nd
Hubback, is Favourite, followed by Punch, Foljambe,
and Hubback, so even 2nd Hubback, is very near
related.   I have now given a rough sketch of the
Duchess's up to 1827 and find Mr. Bates has bred 28
females.   A change here begins to tell the old story,
that too much in, and in, won't do, in 1828 there is
no addition, in 1829, Duchess 29th by 2nd Hubback
is born from Duchess 20th, in 1830, the calves
Duchess 30th, by the same sire, Duchess 31st is also
born to 2nd Hubback, from a second Hubback's dam,

in the year 1831, the same year, also brings a double cross of 2nd Hubback in Duchess 32nd, from Duchess 19th. There only being 4 Duchesses born from the end of the year 1827, up to August 1832.

Prejudice had fought hard for the previous 20 years to gain the mastership by Fashion (in using home-bred sires), but perseverance is of no avail when the battle is lost, experience steps in at Kirklevington, and proclaims himself the conqueror. As Mr. Bates at last opens his eyes to the fact, and travels in search of a bull, in the mean time he takes the advantage of Mr. Whittaker's Bertram (1716), and Gambier, the latter, a son of the former, from a Wildair dam, and full of Mr. Robert Colling's best blood, Bertram was a son of Mr. Charge's Frederick (1060), who had Comet (155), no less than 4 times in his pedigree, and from Red Daisy, bred by Mr. Hustler, by Major (398), if blood like Bertram, and Gambier, was good enough for Messrs. Charge, Whittaker, and Hustler, surely it was good enough for Mr. Bates; but he at last found courage to buy Belvedere (1706), from Mr. Stephenson of Wolviston, a bull equally as well descended as the Duchess's, and tracing further back to the foundation, if that adds anything to the value of either pedigree, or animal; Belvedere was calved April, 1826, consequently in his 6th year, when Mr. Bates bought him, and used him for 6 years longer, so he would be

c

in his 12th year when he was again sold.   Belvedere
was a son of Mr. Stephenson's Waterloo (2816), from
Angelina 2nd, by young Wynyard (2859), a son of
Mr. Robert Colling's Wellington (680), which was
got by Comet (155), from Wildair, by Favourite (252),
Young Wynyards dam being Princess by Favourite
(252), Waterloo (2816), was also by Young Wynyard
from Angelina 1st, by Mr. Robert Colling's
Phenomenon (491), a son of Favourite, Belvederes
gr dam, also being Angelina 1st, by Phenomenon
(491), from Ann Boleyn by Favourite (252), g g dam
Princess, by Favourite (252), g g g dam Colling's
sister to his white bull by Favourite (252), followed
by Hubback (319), the two successive crosses that
Mr. Bates imagined could not be surpassed in the
world.   I trust that I have fully explained that
Belvedere, and the Duchesses, were as one, and the
same in blood, the only difference in the 26 years
that had elapsed since Charles Collings' sale, the
former has but two generations added since that
time, and both these additions are of the Princess
blood, to Mr. Colling's blood of the same line,
apparently Mr. Stephenson, and the Countess
of Antrim, adopted the same course in breeding
as Messrs. Collings, and Bates. Altho' the new bull
to unite with the Duchess is similar blood to themselves, and equally as much in-bred, for a time this
course of breeding will answer, when they are of
different families on the dam's side, however near

related by the sires, I have always found that an impression is made when a male is used from a different family, at any rate, Mr. Bates used his new purchase with confidence to all his animals, and to some, he gave a double cross, one especial result, all Bates breeders will remember in Duke of Northumberland (1940), from Duchess 34th, by Belvedere. I, as well as others must admit, that Mr. Bates was right in his selection, as kindred blood at a distant date, saves the type and constitution, but brothers, and sisters, uncles, and aunts, &c., mated together as Mr. Bates continued to breed after Mr. C. Collings had done before him, it was utterly impossible for such a course of breeding to answer. In August 1832 Duchess 19th calved two heifers to Belvedere (1706), of which one is dead, the following month the 34th Duchess is calved, another 12 months passed, before the 35th arrives, she is by Gambier, the 36th in August 1834, the 37th, in September of the same year, both by Belvedere. In two years, we have but four living Duchesses added, and not a Duke bull, the sire of any of them; so it is evident Mr. Bates felt fully convinced to continue such a course, would be utter ruin, as I find in May, 1835, that Duchess 33rd by Belvedere, produces Duchess 38th, by Mr. Whittaker's Norfolk (2377), a son of 2nd Hubback, tracing through Colling's blood to Hubback (319). I cannot but admire the old gentleman's lingering after Hubback's blood, when

Hubback is no more; to keep him in remembrance, he has his blood in store.   After the birth of the 38th by Norfolk, in the same year, in the months of August, September, and December, Duchess 39th, 40th, and 41st, are all born to Belvedere, as well as the Chief of Kirklevington, or better known as Duke of Northumberland in October of the same year; Short Tail (2621), is calved the year previous to him, and by Belvedere, these are the only two bulls I find recorded from Duchess cows by him, and seven Duchesses, the 33rd, 34th, 36th, 37th, 39th, 40th, and 41st, the 33rd, 36th, and 40th, are from Duchess 19th, by 2nd Hubback. 34th from Duchess 29th, by 2nd Hubback, 37th and 39th, from the 30th, by 2nd Hubback, 41st from the 32nd, with a double cross of 2nd Hubback, from August 1832 to end of December 1835, there were 9 Duchesses made their appearance, besides a dead twin to the 33rd; in addition to Short Tail, and Duke of Northumberland we have Duke of Cleveland, by Bertram, in the last specified period. After this date I find no Duchess recorded until Duchess 49th by Short Tail (2621,) which was calved October 8th, 1839, what became of the 8 intervening ones, I cannot relate anything, except from Bell's History, I find Duchess 42nd, and 43rd, calved in 1837, by Belvedere, and from the 30th, and the 34th, in 1838, and 1839, there are 5 entered to the credit of Short Tail (2621), from the 30th, 34th, and 37th, the 49th, being the only one I can trace any produce

from, being the dam of the 54th, and Earl of Liverpool in the Kirklevingtons, he is by Duke of Northumberland from Duchess 54th by Cleveland Lad 2nd
(3408), Duchess 50th, by Duke of Northumberland
from the 38th, is also calved in 1839, Duchess 51st
is the only one calved in 1840, and by Cleveland
Lad (3907), dam 41st, Duchess 52nd, is by Holkar
(4041), a son of Belvedere, with a dam and gr. dam
both by 2nd Hubback, the dam of the 52nd, is the
38th, by Norfolk, this is the only female in 1842,
in 1843 none at all, in 1844 the 53rd arrived, by
Duke of Northumberland, from the 41st, by Belvedere
followed by a double cross of 2nd Hubback, Duke
of Northumberland is also by Belvedere, dam by
Belvedere, gr. dam by 2nd Hubback, so here we are
again with the close relationship, one thought ere
this, Mr. Bates would have had sufficient experience
in too close alliance, but he tells us that it was not
for profit he bred shorthorns, but for experiment,
surely it is a lesson of experience by experiment,
worth remembering, as we neither see, nor hear any
more of the 53rd Duchess, she is the only one besides
the 50th by Duke of Northumberland. The 55th is
calved in 1844, by 4th Duke of Northumberland
(3649), from the 38th, by Norfolk, the 56th calved
in the same year from the 51st, by 2nd Duke of
Northumberland (3646), the 57th being the only
one born in 1845 is by Cleveland Lad 2nd, from the
50th, the 58th is the solitary calf for 1846, from the

54th, and by Lord Barrington (9308), a son of 2nd
Duke of Northumberland from Lady Barrington, by
Cleveland Lad, gr. dam by Belvedere, the 2nd Duke
has also the double blessing of Belvedere, the 59th,
and 60th, are calved in 1847, the former by 2nd Duke
of Oxford (9046), from the 56th, the latter is by 4th
Duke of Northumberland (3649) from the 54th;
61st, 62nd, and 63rd, are all calved in 1848, and by
2nd Duke of Oxford, from the 51st, 56th, and 54th.
The 64th the last Duchess bred by Mr. Bates, is also
by the same sire from the 55th, and calved in 1849,
the year of his death.   The sale took place on the
9th day of May, 1850, and the following 8 Duchesses
were the only females then living, bred by him, of
which I annex prices realized, and names of
purchasers :—

> Duchess 51st, 60gs., Mr. Bolden.
> Duchess 54th, 90gs., Mr. Eastwood.
> Duchess 55th, 105gs., Lord Ducie.
> Duchess 56th, 52gs., Mr. Ambler.
> Duchess 59th, 200gs., Lord Ducie.
> Duchess 61st, 100gs., Lord Feversham.
> Duchess 62nd, 120gs., Mr. Champion.
> Duchess 64th, 155gs., Lord Ducie.

Should any inaccuracy have occurred in my
explanation of the Duchesses, either in one way or
another, I hope my readers will look upon it as an

oversight, and not wilful mischief, to either the animals as a tribe, or to their previous owners as breeders, the writer fully understanding the difficulties they had to contend with, in procuring sires the early part of the present century ; yet I is not there a fragment of knowledge to be gathered by us, from their errors in breeding, as well as by their experienced judgement, as it is frequently by lessons derived from the former, that the most experience is gained.

CHAPTER III.

THE TRIBES IN MR. BATES' POSSESSION AT HIS DEATH.
OTHER FAMILIES DESCENDED FROM HUBBACK THAT
WERE PURELY DESCENDED, WHICH DID NOT PASS
THROUGH HIS HANDS.

Having briefly described how the Duchesses were
bred in the hands of Mr. C. Collings, and Mr. Bates,
since the first Duchess left Stanwick Park, with the
result of prices obtained, and number of animals in
their possession, at the final dispersion of their
herds, after being bred by them for over a period of
50 years, without effecting any sales to breeders,
beyond the two females sold by Mr. Collings to
Mr. Bates, and the eight animals sold at Kirklevington after his death; the Dukes, that were
descended from the Stanwick Duchess, I will not
attempt to describe, as it is quite probable that
many of them were sold without registration, and
it is not improbable that Mr. Collings and Mr. Bates
might dispose of the weeds to the butcher from the
females, which is undoubtedly the proper course to
pursue, to establish a good tribe, or even a herd of
shorthorns, but this is rarely done without a number
of years visitation from the old master Experience,
although I have no direct proof that this course was
adopted, but whether, or not, the writer shall give
them the credit of doing it, but even if it were so,

the weeds must have been very numerous, or the Duchesses extraordinary slow breeders, seeing there were so few animals of this fashionable tribe at Kirklevington in the year 1850, when we were given to understand that they were superior animals to any other then in existence. If this be a true tale, why were they slow to breed, or why did they produce animals that were not fitted for a better purpose in their youth than the shambles? Surely there must have been something wrong, either in one way, or another, if genealogy in pedigree for half a century is valuable, if not, what is the good of registration at all. I am afraid if the mystery was more fully brought to light, Mr. Prejudice would prove to be the great obstacle that kept the numbers few, at Kirklevington, but stiff-necked as he may be, Experience will at last step in, and claim the victory.

It has been often remarked that Mr. Bates tried many tribes of cattle, but frequently gave them up, and why did he do it? The writer is of an opinion that he had made up his mind to strike out a course of his own, by founding families that he could inter-mingle with his Duchesses, in preference to purchas-ing a male from any other breeder; it is too true that we often prefer mine to thine, and I am afraid it was the case with Mr. Bates. He undoubtedly thought he was better fitted to select a male for his

D

herd than any one else; it is hard to kick against the pricks, for any length of time, no doubt the old veteran began to feel this effect, and departed from singing the song, that all good shorthorns must descend from Hubback, yet prejudice chimes in, they must be full of Hubback's blood, and so the next sires that had the honour of being united to a Duchess at Kirklevington, were Cleveland Lad (3407) and 2nd Duke of Oxford (9046), the former by Short-tail (2621) a son of Belvedere and Duchess 32nd with a double cross of 2nd Hubback (1423), the latter by Duke of Northumberland (1940), with a double blessing of Belvedere, followed by 2nd Hubback, and of course descending from Hubback. The dam of 2nd Duke of Oxford, was Oxford 2nd by Short-tail (2621), consequently own sister to Cleveland Lad. I will at present omit going into the breeding of Cleveland Lad, beyond his sire, to avoid repetition, as I wish to draw my reader's attention in the second part of my experience, why Mr. Bates used him to his Duchesses, yet any observer, might see for himself, that another course of breeding had commenced at Kirklevington, by using the two bulls I have just named, as they were not animals of noble birth, but simply a son, and grandson of Mr. Brown's cow, that passed through Mr. Bell's hands to Mr. Bates for the sum of £11, but why should the descendants of this animal, with two acknowledged crosses of registered blood, be inferior to the descendants of the one, that had previously cost but £13, with one registered cross, when Mr. Collings purchased her at Stanwick Park. It is evident that Mr. Bates saw considerable individual merit in the animal he purchased from Mr. Bell. When the bargain was concluded, he remarked, " I will put her to one of my Duke bulls, and breed a Royal winner," which proved to be the " Oxford Premium cow," by Duke of Cleveland (1987). What was Duke of Cleveland, but a son of Mr. Whittaker's Bertram (1716) from a daughter of Red Daisy, descending from Hubback. The Duke's dam was Duchess 26th by 2nd Hubback, his granddam being Duchess 3rd by Ketton 1st (709). Here we have the best of Bates', Colling's, and Whittaker's blood united to Mr. Brown's cow, by Mr. Bates, who is now a little more cautious through experience gained by breeding Duchesses for experiment not to allow prejudice to overrule his judgment. So here we have a new tribe founded, known by the name of Oxford's, commenced by Mr. Bates, through his own sires and Mr. Brown's cow, but not without being narrowly watched by numerous critics. The old breeder persevered, with prudence, and carried out his object successfully, by breeding 13 cows and heifers in the space of a little more than 10 years. There were 10 females and 3 bulls sold in his sale at an average of £68 16s. each, which proved his judgment on this point to be correct, after 40 years

experience in experimental and unprofitable breeding, through the Duchesses, that all traced to
Hubback.

Mr. Bates commenced the Waterloo family in a
similar way to the Oxfords, by being careful not to
add an abrupt cross upon the preceding Princess
blood, that was derived through the bull Waterloo
2816, which had been used upon his own daughter,
this animal with the double Princess cross, was sent
by Mr. Bates to Mr. Whittaker's Norfolk 2377, a
son of 2nd Hubback, and descending through Mr.
R. Colling's Sally to Hubback, the produce being
Waterloo 3rd, the ancestors of the present Waterloo
family, there being no descendants from Waterloo
2nd by Belvedere, which Mr. Bates tried upon
Waterloo cow, before he sent her to Norfolk.   There
were six animals of this tribe sold in the Kirklevington sale at £59 10s. each, Mr. Bates being the
breeder of twelve of the family, but it is remarkable ·
that he had never used a bull from the Waterloos,
after being in his possession for 19 years, neither
were there any sold in his sale.

The Cambridge, or Red Rose tribe, only supplied
three representatives at the winding up of Mr.
Bates' herd, which resulted in £49 each; what
became of the residue of the descendants from Mr.
Hustler's Red Rose, after 28 years breeding by Mr.

Bates from the foundation commencing with Hubback and of the same family as the idolized 2nd Hubback, I have no information to add beyond that given by Mr. Bell.

The Foggathorpes, another new family in Mr. Bates' hands originally from Mr. R. Colling's stock, had seven animals to represent them, of which four were bulls and realized £46 each. Twenty-five of the prolific Wild Eyes family made £48 a piece, after 18 years breeding from the original cow Wild Eyes, by Emperor (1975) purchased at Mr. Parrington's when a calf in 1831, for 70 shillings, while Red Rose was purchased ten years previous to her, and was supposed to be of a superior type and origin, as she not only descended from Hubback but was the dam of 2nd Hubback.

I have passed over very briefly the families that were in Mr. Bates' possession at the time of his death, owing to Mr. Bell having alluded to them fully in his History of Bates' Cattle, and to avoid much repetition, shall draw my remarks to a close upon the far famed Kirklevington herd, beyond a few hints, that might be useful to the young, or inexperienced, who has not had the privilege of witnessing the dispersion of many representatives from the house of Kirklevington which realized higher prices, than from any other race of cattle on record. The Blanches, and Barringtons are two families that were

sometime in Mr. Bates' possession, but we are not
given to understand by Mr. Bell why they were discarded from Kirklevington, perhaps it was through
the absence of the blood of Hubback, in their
ancestors, but whether this was the reason, or not,
to day, their descendants are equal in personal merit
to any of the six families that were retained as
favourites to build up the experimental herd, that
had taken the best part of a man's life to accomplish
his object, that name will ever oe remembered as a
Hero in Shorthorn History, by the admirers of
Kirklevington blood.

I have dwelt at considerable length upon the
value of Hubback's blood in certain families
through the estimation of Prejudice, but what has
become of the other descendants of Hubback, that
have not had the opportunity of passing through the
critic's hands, where are the descendants of Mr.
Charles Colling's Fortune, the ancestor of Matchem
2281, the grandsire of the first Oxford cow, if Mr.
Bates thought his daughter good enough to breed
a sire to cross his Duchesses surely either he, or
some other breeder, should have seen to preserve
this family in its purity, as a representative of
Hubback; if Mr. Maynard thought Matchem a
desirable exchange for 110gs. at Mr. Mason's sale,
when four years of age, he must have been possessed
of considerable merit beyond being the sire of Mr.
Brown's cow.

If Mr. Bates thought Norfolk 2377 good enough to unite with six of his best females, when in Mr. Whittaker's possession, how is it that this family, being the representatives of Mr. R. Colling's Sally, and descendants of Hubback, have to bow to the offspriug of Mr. Brown's cow; it appears to the writer that prejudice too frequently gained the mastery over prudence in the selection of sires half a century ago, by compulsary measures that they must trace their descent to Hubback, but is this the fashiou in the present day? No! but equally as ruinous to Shorthorns as tracing to Hubback, they must not only trace to either Warlaby or Kirklevington, but have no connexion with the blood of other breeders of the past, they must be line bred in the eyes of the purist. Surely there were men of judgmeut in the early part of the present ceutury, who kuew when they saw a good beast, aud also how to breed one. Are there no pedigrees of sufficieut merit in their purity yet remaining in our herds, that cau boast of descending from such eminent breeders as Messrs. Mason, Whittaker, Wetherell, Maynard, Sir Charles Knightley, Jobson, Wright and Charge, as well as many of their associates, thal are named in the early history upon cattle, whose memories ought ever to be cherished by the admirer of the improved shorthoru, and not to allow prejudice to rule in our minds, that all good cattle must descend

from animals bred by two renowned breeders, who
years ago, took up their abode in one of our North
Eastern Counties.   Do not think for one moment
that I am prejudiced against their style of breeding,
the two both sprang from one root, but branched in
different directions, it is the branches that we have to
cultivate and keep in a prosperous condition, and not
simply to boast that the branches have all one foundation, as in the days of yore, when breeders sang the
song, that all good shorthorns must necessarily
descend from Hubback, or be full of Hubbacks blood,
have I not said enough, to set the old story at nought,
when the descendants of the aristocratic animals have
to bow so low, as to intermix with farmer Brown's
cow, to preserve their fecundity, and prosperity;
shall I not wind up my chapter by saying that
experience has not only fought a victorious battle
against prejudice, but justly conquered, by the aid
of prudence.

CHAPTER IV.

THE EXPERIENCE OF SEVERAL BREEDERS, WITH THE AUTHOR'S REMARKS.

I am áfraid that I shall weary my readers by speaking of Messrs. Collings and Bates, but as it is principally through the tribes that have been in their possession, or full of their blood, that I have had the most experience, it is hard getting beyond what the writer loves to dwell upon most with his pen, and that is a good shorthorn, but it is not necessary it should descend from Hubback. Kirklevington, or Warlaby, it is true, they are musical names in his ears, but all songs do not fit to one tune, neither would the song of Warlaby, or Kirklevington, be a tune of melody in the ears of every shorthorn breeder, so to them he must bid adieu for the present and speak of others whose memory is dear to every true lover of a good shorthorn, and what name could be brought forward more prominently than the late Sir Charles Knightley, who bred shorthorns for pleasure, and built up several families or tribes, by selections from foundations laid by breeders of experience, who were not related to prejudice, neither did they bow to the shorthorn idol known by the name of Hubback, but preferring their own judgement to dwelling entirely upon fashion ; from such breeders

E

as these Sir Charles founded the tribes known as
Rosies, Primroses, Walnuts, Rubys, and the Cold-
creams, have they not been admired and sought after,
yea! and will be again ; good animals, well descended
with sound constitutions, will not be lost sight of
for ever.   The beautiful laid shoulders, and the lovely
countenance that his cattle possessed, which took
Sir Charles the best part of his life to cultivate,
cannot be easily forgotten, their dairy qualities not
neglected by the union of the Earl of Dublin 10178,
the abrupt cross of Duke of Cambridge, with the
idea of gaining a little more substance, taught him
a lesson of experience, by loosing the refined shoulder,
after the in-bred sires that had been in service at
Fawsley Park, it required but a gentle tincture in
memory of Tommy Bates, to have had the desired
effect, step by step, is the proper way to ascend with
safety, to accomplish any improvement required in a
shorthorn. · I need hardly relate that the founder o
these much admired tribes of cattle, suddenly found
that his anxiety to improve their deficiency too
quickly, was but a step backward, as well as that it
took time to gain experience.

Messrs. Becar and Morris, from the U. S. A.,
purchased at Mr. Bates' sale Oxford 5th, by Duke
of Northumberland, as well as her two daughters
10th, and 13th, both by 3rd Duke of York, but
mark the difference in the sires they commence

to use to their new purchases, to what their breeder had done at Kirklevington, apparently their was no studying whether the pedigree traced to Hubback or not. Oxford 5th was put to the following bulls by Mr. Morris, Lord of Eryholme (12205), the produce being a bull, was named Tommy Bates, the union of Samartine (11662), was the next attempt to breed an Oxford, which again proved to be a bull, and was named Oxford Lad, she was next mated with Marquis of Carrabas (11789), the result being Oxford 20th, from which the Maids of Oxford descend, a fourth attempt was made by Mr. Morris to imitate Mr. Bates in breeding, by putting, her to the Marquis of Exeter's Romeo (13619), a bull without any pretensions as to breed, beyond being eligible for the Herd Book, the offspring being a heifer was named Romeo's Oxford, the ancestors of the Oxford Belle's. Oxford 10th, had also the honour of the union of Samartine which proved to be Oxford 17th, the origin of the Belle's of Oxford, but to this daughter of the old cow's, Mr. Morris adds the blood of Mr. Fawkes, though Marquis of Carabas, but fortunately the result of the union was a bull, named Oxfordshire, of which we hear no more. This style of breeding very forcibly reminds me of my own commencement to breed shorthorns, by getting as far wrong as I possibly could in selecting male animals, and surely must have been trying to imitate Mr. Morris, as he appears to have made a blunder

in every calf he bred from his Kirklington purchases, but what is the reason? only one, which is very
easy to explain, that it was for want of experience
alone, and that is a great deal to be deficient of in
commencing to breed shorthorns, as it was by experience that Mr. Bates had bred Mr. Morris' two
Oxford cows. I must not omit to notice what Mr. Becar
was doing with Oxford 13th, he was following in the
steps of his companion by breeding her to Lord of
Eryholme, and Marquis of Carabas, the union in each
case, resulted in a heifer, the one by Lord of Eryholme,
named Maid of Oxford, is the grand-dam of that
beautiful cow Lady Oxford 5th, the ancestor of the
Baroness Oxfords; the daughter of the Marquis, was
named Bride of Oxford, of which we have no further
record, but to the Lady's of Oxfords, and Duchesses
of Oxfords, descended from Oxford 13th, and 2nd
Grand Duke, no cross has ever been admitted since
they left Kirklevington. Three years pass away and we
find Messrs. Becar and Morris at Tortworth Court,
purchasing Duke of Gloucester (11382), for 650gs.,
they have at last had their eyes opened by experience
to see that to breed from fashion on one side, would be
fruitless, consequently the Duke is put to Oxford
13th, and Baron of Oxford is born, one of the hardiest
and most prolific sires ever used across the Atlantic.

Have we not Oxfords that have been bred
in England of Kirklevington fame, that now possess
blood that they would not have done had it not been

for want of experience, have we not many other
Bates families that have blood intermingled with
that of Kirklevington, which would not have been
added had it not been for the absence of experience.
Have we not many other tribes of shorthorns, that
have suffered for want of experience by additions
injudiciously made to the blood they already
contained. Have we not many other tribes gradually
gone to decay, through prejudice gaining the mastery
over prudence by fashion, I may answer safely yes!
and promise that the reason shall be explained in the
second part of my history upon the experiences in
life. What herd was more prosperous, or more gay
in colours, than that of the late Col. Townley's,
between the dates of 1854 and 1864, when at the
latter date it was triumphantly brought to the
hammer by Mr. Strafford at Townley Park, resulting
in an average of £128 for about 50 animals, which
were not distinguishable by Booth or Bates blood
alone, but by a compound mixture, not only of blood
from the two rival houses, but containing a tincture
from almost every leading herd in the kingdom, it
is true, they each had representatives, one by the
Roan Duchess's in descending from Mr. Bates' best
cow Blanche. With a double cross of Belvedere,
and the Pearls from Mr. Booth's Bracelet, as well as
Madaline, by Marcus (2262), it is also true, that the
blood of other great men distinguished as shorthorn
breeders in their day, had a share of honours·in the

production of the successful sale at Townley Park.
The late Earl Ducie of Tortworth Court, contributed
Pride, Pomp, and Parade, the last of the three being
grand-dam of Royal Butterfly's Pagant, the highest
priced animal in the sale, Mr. Betts had to bid
590gs. before he was permitted to take her in
company with the 500gs. Royal Butterfly Duchess,
to Preston Hall, two daughters of Royal Butterfly,
surpassing the prices made of the produce of the
Duke bull, Duke of Wharfdale (19648), and the
Mantalina Baron Hopewell (14134), Barmpton
Butterfly, another daughter of Royal Butterfly and
of the same family as himself claims 350gs. from
Mr. Eastwood.   Double Butterfly, a great grand-
daughter of Mr. Booth's Madaline by the same sire
and her dam, by his own brother Master Butterfly,
realizes 300gs.   Is this not so much due to the credit
of the Barmpton Rose family, having passed through
the hands of Mr. Waldby, Mr. Watson, Mr.
Wetherell, Mr. Eastwood, and Earl Ducie, after
which it was cultivated for years at Townley.   I
have named a few who supplied materials to build
upon, but as yet, have not named the builder, who
built up this herd to such perfection, when the
Butterflies returned from exhibition with many a
laurel upon their heads.   It was no one but plain
Joseph Calshaw, under the guidance in his earlier
days, of the late Sir Charles Tempest and Mr.
Eastwood, Mr. Calshaw was not puffed up by Fashion,

not sold by prejudice, he tried experiments by using
pure Bates, and pure Booth bulls on his Butterflies,
but acknowledged it was not a success, Butterfly
added to Butterfly with a small ingredient of the
result of the work of other experienced breeders in
addition, was his motto, I may take such breeding
as Frederick (11489), the sire of the two famed bulls,
as an example of what the cultivation of the Butterflies achieved, but it was not his breeding alone, but
his produce that gained him favours. After this
famous herd was dispersed, the 6th Maid of Oxford
and Baron Oxford made their appearance at Townley,
along with British Beauty, of the Foggathorpe
family, from Mr. Robinsons of Clifton Pastures,
which bred Baron Oxford Beauty's, that were equal
to their name, the 6th Maid proved to be a bull
breeder, and left no female issue, until after she
went into Gloucestershire, other Barmpton Roses,
were picked up, but for want of pruning in due time
had grown a little wild, they had not the character
of the animals of Townley's cultivation, there was
that want of refinement and gaiety that they originally
possessed, the character once gone, was not easily
restored, not even by the service of such a superior
bull as Baron Oxford, followed by the purest bred
Bates bull in England, they did not reclaim what they
had lost in their absence ; yet the second herd
has also been successfully dispersed by an average
of £121 for 40 animals being obtained, at last the

Butterflies all flew away from Townley Park
when they lighted hither and thither, and have
since had no settled home.

The descendants of the famous Cassandra, by
Miracle (2320), have suffered as much by injudicious
breeding, as the Barmpton Roses, since they left the
supervision of Mr. Culshaw; I remember well, a
grand cow, a daughter of the renowned Frederick,
sent to a bull bred at Warlaby, for the only reason
that he was bred there, the produce being a heifer,
was much more like a camel than a shorthorn in her
shape, this animal came into my possession as I
thought she had a good pedigree, and might breed
something good, so had her put to my own bull,
which resulted in a heifer, comparatively as short in
her legs as her dams were long, not through any good
judgement that I possessed, but simply because I
owned a bull that assisted to restore the Townley
type; this is the way many valuable tribes of cattle
degenerate, passing into such hands as my own,
when scarcely knowing one pedigree from another.
The Cresida's or Cassandra's were the most
fashionable of any family of shorthorns in the neigh-
bourhood where I then resided, I had been told that
Cassandra had bred 3 Royal winners, which sold for
200gs. each, I thought of the honour of winning, but
perhaps more the hopes of obtaining 200 guineas
should I ever be fortunate enough to possess a

descendant of the famous cow, at last my wish was gratified, by purchasing one ; as I intended making money by breeding from her, of course, I put her to a good pedigree, not knowing, or for want of knowledge, did not think that a good animal might be required too, at last a calf was born, which I named Cassandra 3rd, she grew in stature, but scarcely in any other way, she was more like following the hounds, than a shorthorn to be admired, but fortunately another beast jumped upon her and broke her back, this was the end of my experience in breeding Barmpton Roses and Cassandras, but it has not been the end of using my eyes, but perhaps the means of more narrowly watching to see if any other breeders were as ignorant as myself, in knowing how to breed a good shorthorn, alas ! it is too true, that two such families as I have just described, are often condemned unjustly, when the fault rests entirely with injudicious, or inexperienced breeders, these shorthorns degenerate, and are given up with disgust, when the real reason is, that the unfortunate tribes have to suffer, simply for want of experience.

It is still fresh in my memory, travelling with my father in the year 1853, to Holker, to see Oxford 15th, which had just arrived from Tortworth Court, for the sum of 200gs., Mr. Drewery inquired of my father what he thought of his new purchase, the reply he gave, she was worth about £11, so it appears the

F

value of an Oxford was exactly the same amount
when the Duke of Devonshire began to breed Oxfords
as they were when Mr. Bates began 15 years previous.
I was then too young to give an opinion, so had to
be content by keeping my thoughts to myself, as I
have kept them a secret over 30 years, perhaps I may
now be allowed to divulge in them more freely, by
writing of what I can relate respecting the Holker
herd of years gone by, when it was in its infancy ;
but it now has become so gigantic in importance, that
I will not attempt to describe the herd of the
present, but try to picture to my readers what
Holker was in the past, by explaining what has been
done there by experience since I first knew it, when
the Duke of Devonshire, then Earl of Burlington,
and my father vied with each other at the local cattle
shows with their animals.   I remember very dis-
tinctly when there was no opportunity to travel by
rail, that a cow named Rosa, was sent in a covered
cart (called then a caravan), which was dreaded
being seen at the exhibition, as much as the appearance of Bonaparte and his army were in the early
part of the present century.   To win at a local
exhibition was enough for Holker, when I first knew
it.   The families now known as Bracelets, and
Statiras, were then classed amongst the best, and
other families of local repute.   The bull Balco,
bought at Mr. Bates' sale for 150 guineas, was the

first advance towards fashion, but he was shortly disposed of at 80gs. in the first sale at Holker that took place in 1851 and supplanted by Earl of Warwick 11412, which I remember as clearly as if it was but yesterday, seeing him crouching up in a corner more like an unicorn than a highbred shorthorn, he was neither a Master, or a Royal Butterfly in appearance, but an inbred Princess, the sire of "Countess of Oxford," the first female produce of the 200gs. heifer. I have some doubt whether he would have been permitted to occupy the chief place in 1883 as he did in 1853, also whether Priam 18567 would have had the honour of being united to the Earl's daughter in these latter days, when fashion rules almost in preference to judgment. The Holker herd did not attain its present celebrity by chance, or a sudden drop from the clouds, it has risen step by step, through purchase after purchase being made, both in male, and female, from Mr. Grundy of the Dales, Mr. Tanquary, Mr. Maynard, Mr. Mackintosh, Col. Gunter, and others, it has been a work of time and patience, wrought out by experience, to arrive at its present perfection.

I might ramble on with my pen until I had written the last page in the history of my shorthorn experience, describing the doings of great men of the past, and present; of the latter, we have Col. Gunter, who has had the lion's share of good fortune with his descendants from Hubback, and yet he has learned a lesson by Experience that it is not necessary for a beast to descend either from Hubback, or Mr. Brown's cow, to be a true model of a shorthorn. Have we not the name of the late Earl Spencer recorded in the annals of shorthorn history as an influential breeder of the past, was he not a friend, and yet a rival to Mr. Bates, did he not breed the bull Exquisite 8048, that the late Mr. Booth of Killerby and Mr. Torr of Riby, thought good enough to take in exchange for 370 guineas, although the bull was possessed of considerable merit, and descended from the beautiful cow Lady Maynard, the ancestor of Favourite 252, he scarcely answered their expectations, and why, because he did not contain sufficient of the blood of the animals they had selected for his alliance. A male of close breeding, or too far away, are equally mischievous to inbred tribes, an improvement to be made all at once is not as easily accomplished by a sudden change of blood, as an injury might be done; step by step, is the writer's motto, to add fresh blood, a son of Exquisite from a Killerby, or a Riby cow, would have been much more beneficial, but no doubt, Experience taught the purchasers sufficient without any comment from an amateur writer, so I will return and say something more in memory of the late Earl, whom I can remember being talked about as a fashionable breeder when I

was but little more than a prattling child. Spencer,
Mason, Booth, Bates, Wetherell, Whittaker, Maynard and Tempest, were names then often repeated,
and will yet be long remembered. Mr. Mason was
the founder of Earl Spencer's herd, in supplying him
with his best material in Nos. 13, 19, 25, 54 and 57
from Chilton Sale in 1829, from these purchases the
entire herd at Wiseton were descended, excepting
Dairy cows crossed for generations, with Mason
or Spencer blood, until the herd became 130
strong, at the time of its dispersion in 1846, when
several animals made over 100 guineas each. One
purchaser especially, I must not omit to name, that is
the late Earl Ducie, a true lover of a shorthorn, and
who had the boldness to unite the Spencer blood to
the Duchesses, the sudden leap did not meet with
the approval of the purists, neither did it satisfy
the Earl, that his adventure was successful, yet it is
a lesson of experience taught by others for our
benefit, that to add new blood wholesale to inbred
tribes is dangerous. No doubt there were breeders
then, as there are now, that would say, I am not an
admirer especially of Booth, Bates, Spencer, Ducie,
Mason, or Knightley, but an admirer of good cattle,
such a breeder I am afraid is anxious to have all the
praise to himself, as his breeding must descend from
the work of other men's hands; but the writer
would say, give honour to whom honour is due, and
certainly it is due to English breeders of the past,

who have left us a race of cattle not to be equalled by any other nation in the world. May the breeders of the present not only continue to claim, but deserve the championship they now hold by their merit in shorthorn breeding, but it will neither be held by prejudice, nor gained by fashion, but in persevering by prudent selections, in both male, and female, from breeders of experience, no matter whether they are admirers of the blood of Booth, Bates, Mason, Knightley, or any other that have distinguished themselves in years past, by breeding superior cattle. I shall now draw to a close my remarks upon the experience of others, and commence my own history of youth as a shorthorn breeder.

> " Still, I admire the man in silvery gray,
> Who relates the errors of his early day;
> How I love to sit and listen by his side,
> While he describes his mistakes far and wide:
> Not like youth, who thinks himself so clever,
> Appearing always right, mistaken never."

PART II.

CHAPTER L

MY BIRTH-PLACE, MY FATHER'S EXPERIENCE AS A BREEDER, AND THE FIRST IMPRESSIONS IT GAVE ME UPON IN-BREEDING.

Having sufficiently illustrated upon breeders of the past,

"I must not dwell upon Townley's fame,
Or the days that Hubback made his name,"

but return to the days of my boyhood, and inform my readers of my birthplace, and what were the ideas of people in those parts just half a century ago, as it is neither more nor less since I was born, in a pretty village, situated on a hill side, far away from where the writer is now using his pen, sheltered from the cold piercing winds from the North and the East; where the oak and the ash grew luxuriantly, the vine and the fig tree embraced each other beneath the window of the room where I slept. Yes, it was a sheltered and sunny spot, although that village was situated in the extreme end of North Lancashire. The inhabitants there knew nothing of the bustle and hurry of the present day, it was purely an agricultural district, no travelling by rail, nor even the postman's knock to be heard at the door.

How things have now changed, even in that
peaceful little village ; as time rolled on, people from
a distance paid it a visit, and began to talk that a
railway would be a good thing to pass through that
part of the country.   But the inhabitants could not
see what earthly good it could be, as there was
nothing to be carried upon it, neither people to travel
by it ; but at last the task was accomplished.   I well
remember the first train that ran upon it, and so
anxious were the natives to see the wonder of that
age, carriages drawn without horses, that the lame
forgot the assistance of their chief support in help-
ing them to walk.   For years many would not entrust
themselves to be carried by steam, but travelled on
in their old-fashioned way.   The village increased
little by little, until by and by it grew at a miraculous
rate, and a second wonder shortly appeared on the
scene, by a tall chimney being built ; the quiet
residents who had scarcely ever left their native
village, beyond the market town, almost began to
think the tall building springing up so rapidly, to
such an immense height, surely must be a second
Tower of Babel ; but at last they began to see that
it was simply a benefit for their pockets, and that it
would not do for them to stand still any longer, but
to move along with the rest of their fellow-men.

That small village is now a populous and thriving
town, and acres of the land my father owned at the

time is now turned into streets of houses, and even
he altered in his opinion, that land could be turned
to a better account than for agricultural purposes,
just as quickly as he did when he saw that well bred
cattle would be more remunerative than inferior ones.
It was then his practice to buy the weeds from
Ireland in the autumn at £2 each, winter them in
the strawyard, selling them in the spring at about
£4; fortunately for him, there was one of better
quality in the lot, that he was compelled to purchase
at double the amount, but sadly against his wish.
When the spring arrived this high-priced heifer was
sold for £8; which was his first lesson of experience,
that a profit of £4 could be realized by the keeping
of one animal in place of two, so he determined to
purchase the Flower of England in lieu of the weed
from Ireland. As I have said before, there was no
travelling by rail, and seldom by a vehicle of any
kind, so he saddled his horse and went in search of
better cattle, his first purchase being Lady, by
Young Western Comet (1575) dam by a son of
Layton (366) g dam by Layton (366) g g dam Mr.
R. Collings' "Roan Twin," by Simon (590), the
price being about £17. He then paid a second visit
to the same place in Cumberland, and purchased
"Fairy" for £20, by Hetherington Bull (4029), a sire
of the same breed as herself, her dam "Bloom," by
Pilot (496), being bred by the late Mr. Richard
Booth. The horse was saddled once more in pursuit

G

of another good beast into the same county, and
returned after purchasing "Jesamine," also by
Hetherington's Bull, her grand dam being Mr. R.
Booth's "Rebecca," by Pilot, the price of the last
purchase being 25gs.   He had now three well
descended shorthorns to commence breeding from,
but purchasing is not all, knowing what to do
with them is frequently more difficult than purchasing, so the case proved to be with my father ; he had
made good selections to breed from, but let me
explain to my readers how he commenced to improve
upon his new animals in their progeny.   I will
take "Lady" first, as an example.   She was in calf
at the time he purchased her to "Anthony," for
what reason, I could hear of none, only that he was
a very large bull, but without any record whatever
as to his sire or dam ; the produce being the first
shorthorn that my father bred, was named "Ruby
Gilliver."   Although a daughter of "Lady," she
was the daughter of "Anthony" too ; 50 years have
now passed since the error was committed, yet it
remains to this day a blot in the pedigree, and a
stain of the deepest dye to an admirer of purity.

  "Perseverance" joined hand in hand with my
father in his enterprise, but "Prudence" stood afar
off, some might be anxious to know the reason why,
because "Experience" was at a still greater
distance, and surely one error after another will be
committed until they are in unity.   What was

the first blunder the young and inexperienced breeder
made, but sending the refined " Lady " on a visit to
the plain Yorkshireman, a sire without any refinement whatever, or the least trace of his descent. I
could gather no information whatever from him
why she was sent there, only that it was convenient,
and the advice of a neighbour. The production of
the union was a red and white bull, taking in personal
appearance after his dam, a deep and attractive
short-legged animal. He was named " Favourite "
(3772), and so he proved to be one to my father, as
he had his portrait taken and hung up in the hall.
After using Favourite as a sire to all his purchases,
and the connection of " Anthony " with " Ruby Gilliver," makes it appear to the writer rather like a
step backward on the improved shorthorn, but as my
father had not yet gained experience sufficient to
guide him for their improvement, he next permitted
" Lady " to pay a visit to " Stephen " (5324), an
animal even without any local reputation as a sire.
The union of the aristocratic cow and the rustic
" Stephen," resulted in the birth of " Flora." With
this beautiful admixture, I think the young shorthorn breeder was about as well prepared to improve
the breed of shorthorns, as a student to give advice
to a physician, in his first year, how to prepare a
medicine for a patient that is dangerously ill.
" Flora " and " Ruby Gilliver " being the only
daughters of the " Lady," and the old cow herself

has now finished her course, so there is no other
alternative but to breed from the alloyed blood, but
the mischief does not end here.   Sires are used of
their breeding to " Fairy," and " Jesamine," and
for want of experience the descendants of all the
three cows that were judiciously purchased are now
ruined, as far as being purely descended.   What
others had built up, my father had now thrown
down.   He blends the three families together, and
breeds on for a space of 30 years, without even
purchasing a single male animal, but breeds in and
in, one generation after another, until he becomes
somewhat prejudiced against any new blood, closing
his eyes against what was really needed, something
similar to the late Mr. Bates.   A change becomes
compulsory before it is made, and then only in a
small degree, as prejudice and inbreeding allowed
the descendants of Fairy and Jesamine to wear out
until there was not a single animal left in the herd.
But what became of the descendants of " Lady ? "
Why, to-day they are more numerous than ever,
through additions of blood in 10th Grand Duke,
10th Duke of Oxford, and several other influential
sires,   while   the   other   two   families   in   his
herd finished their career nearly 20 years ago, when
they might yet have been numerous and robust
with " judicious " infusions of alien blood, as the
descendants of Lady are better and equally as
healthy cattle as they were half a century back.

I have now spoken of my father as an inexperienced breeder in his youth, as prejudiced in favour
of his own cattle in preference to others, but as yet
have said little in his favour as a breeder in after
life, but others have done it for me, over and over
again, although it may not be in print, it has been
expressed freely from their lips, that he was a
thorough good judge of cattle, and no better manager
of them ever lived; he was exceedingly particular
in their diet and cleanliness, each meal to be given
at a certain hour, I may almost add to the minute,
as well as fresh food given them each time, he was
more particular in breeding good animals than
having good pedigrees, and to some degree prejudiced against fashion. I often begged of him to
get a little more fashionable blood into his herd, but
was soon given to understand that it was all humbug.
He thoroughly enjoyed chatting over the blunders
he had made in his youth, by sending " Lady " to
" Yorkshireman," and Stephen, and often said it
took a lifetime to know how to breed good cattle.
Although his herd was not large, he generally had
not less than three sires for the use of it; as he
truly remarked, no herd could be kept good by the
use of one, but that each male and female should be
mated according to their merits and colours, as the
deficiencies of one might be counteracted by the
merits of the other. I have little doubt but some
of my young readers will be anxious to know

what kind of shorthorns he kept at the time
I have alluded to, I will describe them as
minutely as possible.   What was termed a good
shorthorn then would not be looked upon as a
good one in the present day.   The style of cattle my
father had 35 years ago were genteel enough in
appearance, if not too much so, the head was long,
and narrow.   I remember hearing the herdsman
exclaim, " What a beautiful head ' Rosannah ' has
got, she might almost drink from a quart pot."   No
such exclamation to be heard from the herdsman
in the year 1886.   The breasts of his animals were
wide and deep, somewhat better filled than they are
now, shoulders neat, with deep chest, he had a great
abhorrence of coarse shoulders and narrow chests ;
they were generally deep in the flank, with long
neat hindquarters, but too often rather bare on the
loins, and light in the thighs, by paying too much
attention to the hindquarters, but they were almost
without exception, good at the pail, but not so even
in flesh as the shorthorns are at the present day.

More experienced breeders may be anxious to
know what proof I can give that my father injured
his cattle by inbreeding.   I am afraid after being
an eyewitness for such a length of time, that I am
possessed of evidence sufficient to prove that close
breeding did not improve either animal or constitution.   Year by year, it was my duty to watch the

young animals grow up to maturity, but, alas! it was painful to discern that consumption had found its way to that vital part before the day of maturity had arrived. The eye became dim before their youthful days were passed, and many of the animals gradually sickened and died, without leaving either son or daughter to mourn their loss. Have not there been several other breeders besides him who have sacrificed their herds to inbreeding? What a lesson we have daily before us, in the result of 50 years breeding from the best cow Mr. Charles Colling ever saw, when there were but eight female representatives at the end of that period. Does it not speak volumes against the style of breeding that had been advocated by two of the Prime Ministers of the past, in the shorthorn circle? Where are the descendants of the far-famed Necklace, and Bracelet; where are the descendants of Fame, by Raspberry, free from admixture; I may ask the same question of the beautiful Bliss family, can I not count their numbers upon the fingers of one hand; is it not much easier to put all into one question—Where are all the purely descended families of the late Richard Booth? Why, they are now no more than a tottering reed begging for support from the passer-by. And how has this all come to pass? Simply by prejudice and inbreeding. The latter is good to a certain extent, but I imagine the inexperienced asking to what extent; until the practical

eye of experience observes the animal begin to
deteriorate, but not beyond. Then is the time to
select a change of blood, but to be added as carefully and judiciously as a physician would add his
ingredients to the pure water, before giving it to his
patient, "in hopes of having the desired effect to
restore perfect health." This is the opinion
of the writer upon close breeding of any kind of
cattle, that it may be carried out effectually for
many years by a restorative being given in due season
from the hand of experience, but not to linger until
prejudice lays hold of the constitution.

CHAPTER II.

A PICTURE OF REAL LIFE IN 1846, AND AN IMAGINARY
ONE CONFIRMED IN 1886.

I must ask as a favour from my readers to deviate
a little from shorthorns in the present chapter, as it
is tedious both to the reader and writer to repeat the
same story over and over again, without a little
change, for this reason alone I have selected to write
upon different characters in real life, altho' they
lived before many that may take up this small book,
were born; perhaps I shall not be out of place by
styling them "Funny Folks," why! can I not speak of
people that were peculiar in the past, as well as others
do of people in the present, they speak of shrewd or
ridiculous things being done in our English Capital
by men of renown, but I simply relate in my story
about country people who had no pretensions whatever, not known beyond Mr., or even plain John.
We must all admit that we are now living in peculiar
times, the tenant rebels against his landlord by
informing him that he must have his rent reduced
or he cannot live,

> " As he did in the days of yore,
> Landlord replies, I must have a trifle more,"

H

or I cannot keep my household up to its present
standard. The labourer informs his master

> " That he must really increase his wage,
> To cloth his children up to the present age,"

which causes the labourer to leave his employer and
go complaining about the streets that no employ-
ment is to be had, the master gives up his farm to
his landlord, and endeavours to get him to understand
that the labourer is not worthy of his hire, and
according to present prices of the produce of the land,
his farm is not worth the rent, so the labourer goes
without his wage, the tenant without his farm, and
the landlord without his rent; then the land too
frequently remains in a barren state, neither good to
the unemployed, to a master without his farm, nor
to a landlord without his tenant, surely we are not
living in the brightest of days, but let us live in hope.

But to return to the days of my childhood, when
I was a little fellow prattling by my grandmother's
side, who had the honourable position of being the
Vicar's wife for nearly a period of fifty years, yet she
acted in the humble sphere as the Doctor's assistant
free gratis, in the village where she resided, and as I
named in the last chapter, railways were then few
and far between,

> " So the Doctor complained,
> That his horse was nearly run down,
> Especially when no fee was obtained,
> And even then, it was but half-a-crown.

For this reason the patients became numerous to the assistant, as her medicine was sweet and simple to the taste, which was chiefly composed of juice from the honey-comb, tinctured from the long necked bottle, her advice kindly and cheering, and often adding with it, take that home with you, it may be found useful, so naturally the patients flocked to the parson's wife, in preference to the doctor, because they said she was more clever, and I agreed with them, as she slipped many a bright piece of silver into my hands, that even my brothers did not observe, young as I was then, I thought how nicely she had done it, and how wisely the inhabitants spoke when they called her clever, yes! self is an old man full of years, but free from honour.

The next persons that I shall speak of, are Mr. and Mrs. Thrifty who resided in the same village, and probably partook of the same hospitality. There was then a small estate to sell by auction measuring about seventy acres, within a few yards from my grandmother's door, the auctioneer announced that the last bid of £900 fell from the lips of Mr. Thrifty, and if no advance was made, the estate would become his property, so at last he declared the purchaser to be Mr. Thrifty, adding, kindly give me a substantial name, that the money will be forthcoming when required, but almost with a sneer upon his countenance, doubting if the purchaser could find one. Mr.

Thrifty had by this time received quite enough of his
chaff, when he knew he held the grain in his own hands,
as well as the chaff, turning round to his wife, and
speaking in affectionate terms; "Now Katie, where's
thy bondsman," Kate had only to remove her apron,
and the bondsman appeared in the shape of a stocking,
well secured by needle and thread, the latter was rent
asunder, and the bondsman immediately made his
appearance by 900 sovereigns being poured upon the
table, in payment of the estate, Thrifty knavely
replying, it was the only bond that he had to offer.
What a difference then, to a sale of property in the
present day, there is rarely an estate now to be sold
without Lawyer, Mortgagee, and Mortgagor having a
finger in the pie, but not so with Mr. and Mrs. Thrifty,
it was the substance of the toil of their long life, and
they had no desire for any one to share the estate
with them, while they could enjoy it. It was rented by
Mr. Grumbler, at £50 per annum, until his retirement
from public life, if I may be allowed to use such an
expression, and I think I have good grounds for doing
so, as I often had a chat with him in his last earthly
dwelling place, which was rented at £4 per annum,
and the only entrance to it was from one door, facing
a large rock, and if I could compare him to anything
at all, it would be to that grim rock, as I never
remember seeing even one smile pass over his face,
and to see it in that house, after the bright rays of
the sun had passed from the sky, would have been

impossible, as the writer never distinguished a light burning within that door, nor the least signs of brightness upon the occupier's countenance; this is one way of retirement from public life, but I should not say a happy one; allow me just to explain the result of a portion of the sale of his farm stock. His ewes in lamb averaged about thirteen shillings per head, and the Auctioneer remarked he thought they sold remarkably well for the times, four two year old heifers which the writer can remember individually realized the following prices, sixty-six shillings, fifty-six, fifty-four, and forty-two shillings respectively, it remains for my readers to judge, whether we have more reason to complain of the farming of to-day, or the farming of forty-four years ago.

By this time both Mr. and Mrs. Thrifty had passed away from us, and the estate had fallen into the hands of Mr. Spendall, who enjoyed himself thoroughly after his own fashion, altho' persevering in everything he undertook, and as I explained in my last chapter, a railway was just completed in that locality, of course he must travel by steam, as the old fashioned highways were a thing of the past for men of business, evidently he was as much too fast, as the late owner was too slow, he started his journey in life as if nothing would ever come to an end, and eventually travelled on the wrong line, and booked for the most fashionable station then in existence, but let me not

forget to add, Mr. Prejudice was his too frequent
companion, and strongly advised him not to take a
ticket for the quiet little town of Prudence, where he
should undoubtedly have travelled, but Mr. Spendall
at last travelled on and on until he came to the end
of his journey, which was in the town of Fashion,
where he had a desire to reside, a stranger met him
there, kuown by the name of Experience, and very
politely informed him that £2,000 was too weighty a
matter to rest upon the contents of a stocking, and
requested that a portion of its burden, if not all,
would shortly be removed. This is another lesson of
experience learned by the writer, that ueither Fashion
nor Perseverance cau profitably exist without Prudence aud Experience. Honest John was a labourer at
the time in the same village, who had to be content
with five shillings per week, for his family's support.
Stout hearted David a little more capable as a work-
man, often admitted that seven shillings for six days
toil was canny pay for his labour. Farmer Saveall,
his employer, knew that the extravagaut wage would
be well earned, before he parted with it; as he is the
last of the list of my "Funuy Folks" for 1846, I
must not close without makiug a few remarks,
respecting his peculiarities, he imagined he was not
very strong, and could not partake of anything that
was very rich, as he had a weak stomach, but neighbour Prudent invited him to dine with him; poor
farmer Saveall quite forgot his weak stomach, and

expressed himself how happy he could be if he only
lived with gentle folks. He provided the food for
his cattle six days in a week, and thought they were
to some extent like human beings, requiring rest
from their labours; as he was a man that did not
care for theory, but approved of his ideas being
carried out practically, especially when it suited his
pocket, so he allowed their stomachs to rest on the
seventh day, and said surely they can not give up
thriving for lack of one day's food,

> " He made his calculations so fine,
> That he never asked a neighbour to dine,
> For fear he should not have enough for tomorrow,
> And bring upon himself nothing but sorrow."

I have spoken of Messrs. Saveall, Spendall, Grumbler,
and Thrifty, as a sample of funny folks, bordering
upon half a century since I first knew them, had they
been living in the present day with their peculiarities,
they would have been looked upon as almost insane.
The picture that I have drawn upon my experience
from real life, of the above characters, may appear to
some of my readers without any aim at any object,
but if they are under that impression, I trust they
will find that they are slightly mistaken before the
close of the chapter, as the drawer of the picture
gives his assurance that it is full of meaning to them
that study it with the keenest eye, or even in comparing the difference of life between now and forty

years back, it simply requires touching up with the
accomplished artist's brush and placing within his
gilded frame,

> " Then I feel it would be much admired,
> Full of meaning and greatly desired."

Having completed my picture upon the peculiarities
of 1846, I will next try to compare an equal number
of imaginary characters of 1886, to the reality of the
earlier period, and perhaps some of its admirers
may agree with the painter that there is a similarity
between the two, altho' forty years have elapsed since
the former picture was drawn.　To commence the
latter drawing, I must first compare notes with Mr.
Grumbler of to day, and the one of forty years ago,
in personal appearance they might be brothers, in
actions nearer still, if it is possible to be so, he is an
unthankful servant, a disagreeable master, and not an
amiable landlord, for any one to have to contend
with, he is continually complaining of the times, the
weather, or his tenantry, and rarely agreeing with
himself twelve hours together; I should much like
to have put him behind the scenes in my imaginations,
but no, such a character must be placed in the front
ranks for exposition, but I shall only place him on
the left side of my drawing and put near him his
friend Mr. Saveall, he too I willingly would have
driven from my thoughts, and placed him also in the
background, but it would not be fair to screen him

from public notice, as he is a mean fellow, and thinks
of no one but himself, therefore I shall bring him
forward and expose him to his friends, but doubt
very much if he has many, so I will leave him alone
for the present, and introduce Mr. Spendall, who I
will let stand at the bottom of my painting, for fear
he should injure himself by falling, if I place him
higher, as it will surely be his destination, sooner or
later, unlike Mr. Saveall, he remembers every one
but himself in his kindness, he is what many term a
jolly good fellow. Standing higher in the picture is
Mr. Thrifty, apparently looking very grave at the
three characters I have already represented, that one
should appear so reckless, another so mean, and a
third so prejudiced against any improvement in
society, he therefore quietly removes the piece of clay
from between his lips, and inquires the reason they are
so sad. Mr. Spendall replies that he had invested
his all in the Town of Fashion, and the only thing
that troubled him was, who would receive the interest,
Mr. Grumbler's and Mr. Saveall's troubles were as
one, they replied the times were really so bad, that
they could save no more, and that the eminent Mr.
Whitewash had thoroughly deceived them by prom-
ising that they would improve for the last seven
years, and they were not one jot better now, than they
were then, but worse than that, they understood by
his gifted speech and flowery language. that he would
have all the land divided into equal portions, and

I

that there would be no reason either to grumble or
save any more, so we freely supported him. When
shortly after he retired into the Forest and quite
forgot either his promise of the good times, or the
division of the land. Mr. Thrifty who had now to
take the name of Perseverance, through a legacy being
left him by the will of Prudence, cast his eye upon
the gentleman in the centre of the picture, whose
name is Experience, and exclaims there's the man
of Solidity, call at his office in Salisbury Square, and
you will find Mr. Prudence awaiting to receive you
at the door, and Mr. Perseverance prepared to assist
you on the way to prosperity. Mr. Saveall on hearing
the good news, could hardly contain himself for joy,
and made up his mind to put his scraping machine in
order, so that he might die worth another thousand,
look at the thin and miserable face he has got,
compare it with the gentleman's at the right side of
the picture, one might imagine that he had lived all
life long in the height of prosperity and happiness,
while the former is fretting and fuming over his
nephew John, who has not married according to his
liking, therefore he must cut him short in his will,
yes! that is the punishment for his nephew's dis-
obedience. His niece Mary has also displeased him
by marrying a scamp, that entitles her to be left
ont in the cold, and her poor sister Elizabeth, has
disgraced herself by being too extravagant, as she
gave a shilling away to the poor where sixpence

ought to have done, she is not to be trusted with much money, therefore it gives the old Uncle the trouble of again altering his will, and see that she cannot either give or spend too much. Poor fellow, what anxiety he brings upon himself, but it is some consolation when he hears that his nephew Solomon is making money very fast, by following in his steps, it appears most probable that Benjamin's share of the hard savings shall fall to his lot.

Mr. Grumbler also tries to raise a smile on hearing the good news of returning prosperity, but alas! they are no glad tidings for him, as he has spent the best part of his life in being prejudiced against any improvement being made for the welfare of his fellow-men and declares he has been one of the most unfortunate beings in existence, as he has always been industrious and most careful, or perhaps the writer may add greedy to the extreme, he thinks if he had been as fortunate as his neighbours, he would have had, at his time of life, a good round sum to have made a respectable division at his death for his family, but for some reason or other his sons had not helped him to gather, but rather to scatter, and that last law suit also cost him a considerable sum, which was only one of a few, through squabbling over trivial matters, and it very often rained when he wanted to secure his crops, which caused them to be sold at a low price, and his stock rarely made so high a figure as

that of his neighbours, and the times are really so bad
that there is little hope of ever doing any more good
in farming at all.   Mr. Spendall is apparently
in high spirits, when he hears it is probable that he
may once more return to his former position in life,
by the improvement of the times, the old centre
piece of the picture whispers in his ear, improve
thyself with the times, the hint is not thrown away
upon Mr. Spendall, as he has had enough of the advice
given him by Mr. Prejudice and Mr. Fashion that he
now gladly travels by the line of Perseverance, to
commence business in the town of Prudence, where he
receives a healing balm for his bruises, and a permanent cure for his fall.   But not so with Mr. Grumbler,
nor Mr. Saveall, the former appears to the painter to
be a hopeless case, as he finds it impossible to draw
his face straight for his picture, it may be that Mr.
Prejudice has allowed him to hold it for so many years
in that crooked position, or perhaps the climate has
something to do with it, as he generally takes up his
abode in the extreme North of our British Empire,
where the frosts are very severe, which may have left a
hard impression upon it, but as I am only an amateur
in painting, I shall leave the mystery to be unravelled
by a more experienced hand.   But just one more
touch up with the brush before finishing my imaginary
work of 1886, as I feel certain I could improve Mr.
Saveall's face by a little more paint, as it is the most
miserable looking in the whole group, the more out

of sight it is kept the more it is admired. Altho' he dwells in the far west, he cannot get away from his troubles, his nephew Solomon, undoubtedly very rich, has at last displeased him, by driving his carriage, which he thinks not only a very expensive, but unnecessary habit, his misdemeanour causes the will to be altered once more, to see that his nephew is bound to maintain the family position in life, by his walking on foot, and not to forget that his name is Solomon Saveall. The old man now begins to get weary of nephews and nieces, as they are continually trying to get from him what he prizes most, so he makes up his mind to do good with his money, when he is bound to part with it. At last the time comes when the machinery of life stops, the last will and testament of the late Mr. Saveall is read, to the disappointment of all nephews and nieces, when they hear that all the scrapings of a long and weary life are left to an entire stranger, and the name of that stranger is "Charity." Kindly admire the contented looking face of Mr. Thrifty as he is making his speech from the gallery, he has risen little by little through Prudence and Perseverance until he now holds a high position in life, watch how he pushes away old Mr. Whitewash from him, as he hovers about the crown of the picture, and adds, he may hover round about it, but shall never enter within its frame. There's the man of Experience in the centre, he exclaims, he shall be the leader of the party to restore England to its former greatness, there stands his chief supporter on the right, " Prudence " by name and nature, a friend to the landlord, tenant, and labourer, three important persons of the past, present, and future, the prosperity of the nation cannot move on without them, so be of good cheer landlord, tenant, and labourer, brighter days are in store for you, and are now in the bud. I shall now lay down my brush with the satisfaction of knowing that a painter of even an imaginary picture requires experience before his work can possibly be made perfect.

See Page 201.

CHAPTER III.

WISDOM IN YOUTH, ADVICE HOW TO UNITE MY
EXPERIENCES, MY FIRST SHORTHORNS, GAINING
EXPERIENCE BY BEING A DISAPPOINTED EXHIBITOR,
MY FIRST SALE, OR PRELIMINARY EXAMINATION,
HAVING THE VILLAGE SCHOOL FOR THE PREPARA-
TORY.

Having passed over briefly, in the two last
chapters, the days of my childhood and boyhood, I
must now advance with my experience a step
forward to the time of early manhood, a point in
life when the young man thinks himself possessed
of wisdom to overflowing, but when he has advanced
so far in life as to see another generation take his
place in youth, he looks back with regret upon his
early wisdom, although he has now spent half of
his allotted time, he feels anxious to gain more
knowledge, and is convinced that it only can
be obtained by experience, at any rate it is the case
with the writer, who has been asked to write a book
upon his experience in life, but to dwell principally
upon shorthorn breeding; the request has been granted
to the best of his ability, but he feels sure that he
is not capable of meeting their desires upon every
point, so has made up his mind to compose this

small volume in his own style, which his future
readers principally know must be an old-fashioned
one; but if he can avoid it the book shall not fall
from any one's hand and say that he had written
them to sleep, but on the contrary, will try to
awake them out of it, not by praising their cattle,
or their doings, but by showing the folly of fashion
in shorthorn breeding without experience, and for
want of the latter the writer did not know when to
accept the benefit of the former.   It is perfectly
true that he has been requested to write a book upon
his experiences; but, more than that, advised how
to write it, not only once, but over and over again.
The first says write it all upon shorthorns, as you
have had considerable experience in them; another
tells him not to write it all upon shorthorns, but
intermix it with other experiences in general; a
third requests that it should not be written too dry,
or the people will never read it; his companion
advises differently, and says don't write as you talk,
but put it more seriously; a fifth presents more
liberal terms by adding, don't be too grave and
serious with your remarks, but give it a jovial turn
so that the reader may compliment the writer; but
the sixth adviser is perhaps the most suitable to both
writer and reader, as he desires that the book
should be a sensible one.   Yes, I believe he is right,
to a certain extent, if he bears in remembrance that
what is sensible to one is not to another ; but I am

a little afraid that prejudice in his case might get the master of prudence, and not allow a sufficient margin for different opinions, although I must not forget the old man who carried his ass to please every one. Yet, it is by different opinions collected together, and well sifted, that we gain knowledge, and that is not to be gained only by small proportions in one day; as I have repeatedly said, it requires time and experience to be anything near perfect, even if it be only in the writing of a small book. So there is room for excuse in an amateur writer, as much as there is in an inexperienced shorthorn breeder; fortunately I shall be a shareholder in both, as the blunders made in the commencement of my career as a breeder were numerous, but perhaps more amusing than the losses I sustained by them.

As a writer I do not claim any pretensions whatever, but simply express myself in such language as any youth might understand. As a painter I acknowledge my drawings are not very clear, and rather difficult to discern the characters they represent, especially to those who do not care to understand them.

I must now return to the year 1860, when I commenced farming, as I had then become a master, naturally thought myself fitted to instruct others, and as I was most active with my

K

fect and tongue, imagined I could not be far
behind my seniors in knowledge upon farming, so I
was determined that I would not be left behind, and
entered my farm for the prize, being the best
managed throughout; there were three competitors,
and three prizes; the young farmer had the honour
of distinguishing himself by gaining the third prize;
this was a gentle hint that he was somewhat behind the men of riper years, who had gained their
knowledge by time and experience.

Being fond of cattle, I soon made up my mind
to surpass my neighbours there also, and had heard
that to get good cattle they must be well-bred, so
desired that my father should present me with one
or two with pedigrees; to oblige me he did so, and
purchased from Mr. Caddy, of Rougholm, in Cumberland, a cow called Buttercup 3rd, and her heifer
calf Buttercup 4th, the price being £23 the pair;
they were such cattle that I recommend in my
introductory chapter, suitable for any breeder that
has rent to pay for the land he occupies; but not
being satisfied with the breeding of such animals
as he previously had deemed prudent to give me, I
imagined as I had now become a man, that I understood shorthorn breeding as well as he did, so I readily
made up my mind to follow in the steps of his
youth, and go in search of better bred cattle; at
last I purchased a heifer at the same home, and

descended from the same cow Jesamine as he purchased about 30 years previous; I had my new bargain brought home with considerable glee, as I considered her better bred than any that he possessed, the price being £10 at two years of age; my father came over to see the new and important purchase; he was so long in giving his opinion upon it that I asked him the reason, he replied he was just looking to see if she was a heifer at all; I felt a little annoyed at his decision, and therefore decided to follow my own course in the way that I would breed from her, so in due time she was put to Belvedere (23405), a bull bred from Buttercup 3rd, by John Bunyan (20030), descended from Jesamine, and full of the blood of the renowned Stephen, and Yorkshireman, mentioned in the previous chapter, where I spoke of my father's ridiculous breeding, and what was I now doing but adopting the same course as he did then, simply for want of experience? The produce of the union resulted in a white heifer, which I named "Princess Helena," thinking I must imitate in a fashionable name if I could do nothing more, her dam was "Princess Alice," a grand-daughter of Mr. Booth's "Baron Warlaby," and as I explained before, Jesamine was a grand-daughter of Mr. Booth's "Rebecca," therefore I had a good foundation to build upon, but destroyed the structure already made, by the birth of "Princess Helena," although she was a Princess, and daughter of "Princess Alice," I was often reminded that she was the daughter of Belvedere too; what a blunder to make by one that had thought himself fully capable of finding fault with others. "Princess Helena" being a pretty little creature, although somewhat diminutive looking, I made up my mind to exhibit her for the prize, which she won easily in a large class, so easily, that it stole away the judgment of its owner. The following year she was again exhibited; of course, I felt quite certain that there would be nothing there to equal her, but to my horror, the lovely Princess was left in the background, not that I thought she was deficient in beauty, but the judges did not understand their business, and awarded the prize to the wrong animal; this was my first lesson of experience that animals were not brought before judges at a Show for them to point out their merits; no! they are already known by their owners too well, but they are placed before them as a criminal at the Bar is placed before a Court of Justice, to find out where they are wrong. I had not thought of this before, but a lesson from the book of experience teaches one that wisdom in youth is but little more than folly. I had so far made no improvement upon what others had done before me in their breeding, as I next put her to a bull of the Elvira family, and lastly to a pure Bates bull, which was about as far in the wrong direction as I could possibly get.

Let me briefly explain what became of Buttercup 3rd, and her descendants which I bred for generations without any aim as to pedigree, beyond that they were eligible for the English Herd Book, the pedigree read as follows, by Flying Dutchman (10235), by Bachelor (5770), by Esk (23895), by Coroner (3497), I had not as yet been taught beyond the alphabet in shorthorn knowledge, so imagined they were equally as valuable, as the animals of accomplished breeders, but many a hard lesson must be learned by the inexperienced, before he can stand in the front ranks as a breeder, at least the writer had many difficulties to contend with before he even passed his preliminary examination. The Buttercup family, altho' fairly good in themselves never left their mark beyond their own locality; so I decided to give them up; and the descendants of Princess Alice, I had utterly taken away the most profitable and interesting part of their history by injudicious crossing, as they were lineally descended from fashionable ancestors.

> Fashion, added to fashion, is a dangerous game to play;
> Judgment, added to fashion, is sure to gain the day.

But I am sorry to say I was not guilty of either of the two, as I neither added fashion nor judgment to the descendants of " Princess Alice," but simply prepared them fitted for nobody. What could I have done more? I imagined as I had persevered with all my might in breeding shorthorns since my commencement. I had now an offer of £27 10s. for the old Princess, which I gladly accepted, thinking there could not be much benefit remaining for any one else, after receiving such an exhorbitant price, leaving in my hands her two daughters and a grand-daughter. A little more than two years elapsed when she was again sold for 42gs., and her daughter realizing 80gs. What a lesson this taught me, that even "Princess Alice" in experienced hands was capable of breeding valuable animals; and what were her other daughters in comparison? They were simply daughters of sires descended from "Folly," a very prolific family in my herd; so I made up my mind to dispose of them all at the first opportunity, and purchase animals from the tribes of "Fashion," and see if I could not make some improvement, as up to this date I could only give myself the credit of removing the improved shorthorn a step backward, I had so far been disappointed in not securing the best of blood, as I imagined, by keeping too near ashore. So I ventured a little further out from land, and succeeded in buying, or rather Mr. Thornton succeeded in selling me, three Blanche cows, and one of the J. tribe. After these important purchases, my pride and wisdom increased immensely upon shorthorn matters, when a neighbour inquired of me if I had not purchased some shorthorns, I replied yes; he

added, he meant real shorthorns, not simply animals
with pedigrees; my further reply was, he was quite
right, they were real ones. My friends came far
and near to see these extraordinary animals, and no
doubt I disclosed my wisdom to no few, and to their
astonishment my ignorance in the breeding of shorthorns. As to the J. cow, I did not then know she
was descended from Princess, by Favourite (252);
I was not even then possessed of a very large percentage of herd book knowledge, or I would not
have been prevailed upon to buy animals seeking a
customer, but lessons must be taught us before we
thoroughly understand that experience is so great a
master. I must confess that this lesson opened my
eyes, to a certain extent, when I found the young
and bright London auctioneer had used his persuasive powers so successfully in disposing of three
of the most indifferent bred Blanches then in existence, and the J. animal one of the meanest-
looking brutes I ever saw, I almost began to doubt
if she was a real shorthorn at all, but simply an
animal with a pedigree, like hundreds of those that
Mr. Fashion has purchased since,

At a more costly price in pounds, than two score;
As this was the price of each Blanche, and nothing more.

In addition to the above purchases I secured many
animals of local reputation, besides giving 50gs. for
a bull of the Fletcher tribe, which proved quite a
success, and became the sire of many good animals.

My herd having now increased considerably, and prefering some other persons owning a portion of them to myself, as I had begun to take lessons upon breeding, and found when my pedigrees were analised, that they scarcely contained 50 per cent. of what I wanted. What was the next course to adopt, but to dispose of some of the animals by applying to the same gentleman in London, who gave me his advice so freely in purchasing them. He now advises me to sell by auction ; so I partook of the advice given, for the second time, and advertised my first shorthorn sale to take place on the 21st day of September, 1871, by John Thornton, which resulted in an average of £30 a piece for thirty head, which was considered a very satisfactory examination for a preliminary to being a shorthorn breeder, after the serious blunders I had made in the alphabet, but dull beginners sometimes advance more quickly with their lessons as they grow in years than the brightest youth, who rushes along without having them thoroughly grounded. I must close my chapter, at the time I had to leave the village school to go to another, as a preparatory, for a fashionable shorthorn breeder ; so bid good bye to Mr. Experience until we met again, as I was then in haste to meet my new master, and had but very little time for studying before I went in for the next examination.

CHAPTER IV.

GAINING EXPERIENCE BY EXPENSIVE PURCHASES UNDER THE GUIDANCE OF FASHION. PASSING THE INTERMEDIATE EXAMINATION BY A SECOND SUCCESSFUL SALE.

Feeling a little languid and weary after the exertions of the public examination, it was natural one required a little rest, and as the days were short and dreary, I gave up studying until after Christmas holidays were past, when I felt more sure that I could then go to work in earnest, and as I had but little over a year to prepare for the intermediate, there was no time to be lost, yet preferring lingering on to the spring, before commencing my arduous task, when it would be more cheering, and often new ideas spring up in one's thoughts, as bright as the morning sun. But further excuses were useless, as my new master was at hand, whose name was Mr. Fashion, who kindly invited me to go into work, and so to work I went at once, and to inform my readers what I did, and how I did it, I think it best to return back to the previous midsummer, or to explain my doings more minutely a little further still, to the time that the writer loves most, and that is the spring.

L

It was a pleasant and sunny afternoon for my journey, when I travelled a little to the west, the day was drawing to a close as I arrived at my destination, where I accomplished the work Mr. Fashion had sent me to do, and that was, to purchase a bull calf for the sum of 150gs. My neighbours and friends seemed thunderstruck at the idea, and exclaimed such like work could never pay, fifty guineas profit was offered before the traveller's return, could such a thing be, they asked one another, in reply to their own question, they answered themselves, if he has refused such a profit, he surely must be insane, the animal, which was an Oxford, arrived safely at home, and was much admired in every respect but his price ; but allow me to pass on and leave the mystery for the present, as I have other work to explain.　The year advanced from Spring into Summer, when I took a second journey as pleasant as the former, to where I spent an enjoyable evening with Mr. Thomas Bell, who entertained me by describing the animals he had so often admired in the possession of Mr. Bates, it is pleasant to chat over with experienced men their doings of the past, it prepares a young man to look forward in the hopes that he should some day distinguish himself as a breeder. The old veteran informed me the same evening that Kirklevington 10th was the best animal of that family bred up to that time, and that Kirklevington 24th, a grand-daughter of hers, was to sell the follow-

ing day, at Messrs. Harward and Downings sale, so I
made up my mind to go and purchase her; the last
sand passed from the glass as the writer's bid stood
at 100gs.; a cheap calf was the exclamation round
the ring, a very pretty one indeed; the animal
was sent to my farm and prospered; but its owner
has omitted an important purchase which he previously made when he travelled in a southern
direction, but on a cold frosty night at the end of
March, when the wind was piercing, and company
scarce, but he had an object in view, so travelled on
until he was gladly released from his cold habitation,
and drove out to the late Capt. Olliver's, and there
had the pleasure of inspecting Grand Duchess 17th,
and her descendants; it was there he learned that a
highly-bred shorthorn was considered a good milker,
when she gave but half the quantity of what the
animals did he had left behind him; but on to the
end of his journey he must travel, as Mr. Fashion
had sent him on a mission, where he arrived at
early morn, and was greeted by Mr. Robart's, the
banker, and the owner of the cattle for sale. The
traveller made the purchase he went in search of,
and that was "Lady Barrington 9th," a very pretty
red heifer seven months old, for the sum of 77gs.
Grand Princess, a neat red cow, of the Darlington
family, accompanied her, but unfortunately broke
her leg, without leaving any issue. One year
passes quickly after another, as it was on a busy

morning with me in the following spring that a
perfect stranger, a gentleman from a northern
county, drove up to my door, inquiring if he could
have a peep at my shorthorns. I was delighted to
show them to him, especially when he came from so
great a distance, but perhaps for a better reason
still, he asked me what I had to sell, that was something new to be asked by a stranger; before the
day had closed the animal that I was condemned
for buying, was sold for 300gs.; the ordinary looking
J. cow, and her heifer calf at 80gs.; a Kirklevington
heifer calf, of my own breeding, 70gs., at four
months old; and a pair of young bull calves at 65gs.
I felt sure I was right when I admired the spring
in preference to winter. Notice what one bargain
brought forth on that lovely spring day; my
neighbours could not admire it as I did, but simply
said I was a lucky fellow. I did not understand
whether it was for selling the cattle so well, or for
escaping insanity, if I had not sold them ; whether
sane or not sane, I again travelled by rail and
purchased two animals of the far-famed Kirklevington blood, male and female; but the former a
friend of mine induced me to give up for a small
profit; the latter was one of the prettiest of pretty
ones, but what a price 300gs. for Kirklevington
Duchess 7th, and only seven months old; surely it
can never pay, was the remark of Mr. Prejudice and
his friends.

I had by this time three Kirklevington females, and one Barrington, but no male for my herd, so I had again to travel south, in pursuit of a bull, which proved to be an Oxford, a better animal at less price than the one I had sold, but his produce scarcely proved equal to his appearance, although a daughter of his afterwards realized 265gs.; she was not such an animal as Mr. Experience would approve of, but the junior master, Mr. Fashion, would gladly accept her for a good heifer, as she was fashionably bred, and possessed of an attractive appearance.

Up to this time I had been most particular in selection of good animals, and the three red calves that I had purchased would bear inspection by any critic as to personal merit. So far Mr. Fashion had not been allowed to draw me away from carrying out practically what Mr. Experience had previously taught me. As yet my two masters agreed in their teaching for me to buy fashionably bred animals, and I feel certain that their pupil was most obedient to their instructions, at least, as near as it was possible, 1 obeyed two masters in every point, but if any favour was shewn at all, it was towards Mr. Fashion, as Mr. Experience was so very particular and exact in everything, the animal must be perfect, pedigree good, and the constitution faultless ; not so with Mr. Fashion, he

let me off much easier, if the animal was fashionably bred, of a taking character, and not actually
under the veterinary treatment, it would do ad-
mirably for him, and I am afraid his pupil too.

By this time I had a herd of shorthorns that
people began to talk and write about; it is a very
easy matter for an inexperienced breeder to listen
to the varnished description given of his herd in
some local paper written by an unpractical writer,
the temptation is strong enough for him to believe
it is real, and imagine that his herd is much
superior to his neighbours, but public opinion will
decide the matter for him when required, if it be to
find their money value, and it is to that value we
must aim if we desire shorthorn breeding to pay a
fair percentage for the outlay; that has been, and is
still the writer's aim, whether in breeding pedigreed,
or nonpedigreed animals, fashionable, or animals of
lower degree, to go on improving our herds from
the foundation is the point not to be lost sight of,
but how few do it in youth for want of experience,
or rather by being in too great haste after fashion?
Has not the writer said enough respecting the
blunders of his early days? but he will say still more
before he closes the volume of his experience upon
shorthorn breeding. Kindly allow him to relate
how he was spending his leisure hours at the close
of the year 1872. Why, he was as busy as Mr.

Fashion could possibly make him in preparing his
lessons for the following spring, when the intermediate would take place, there was no more
freedom to be had until that difficulty had been
overcome.

The herd had now increased so much by purchases
and births that it was really necessary to reduce it;
to leave it more select, there were many weeds to
be plucked out before it could be classed as the
most fashionable. A fashionable master, with perseverance, will compel his pupil to accomplish his
lesson however difficult; this left him no alternative
but to fix a date for the next examination, and as
there was a rising tendency for well-bred shorthorns, he thought there was but little fear he should
get him through easily; but Experience thought
differently, and said, so little had been done to improve the animals of my own breeding of late in
appearance, it would require all the assistance that
could be obtained from Prudence and Perseverance,
to pass successfully on the 8th of April, as that was
the day fixed for the inspector of the highest
authority upon Bates cattle to attend at Ulverston,
when, and where, my herd must undergo the
strictest examination; after due notice had been
given, I set to work and prepared in earnest for the
event. Mr. Strafford (from London) was the name
of the inspector, and the place where he would

attend was Mr. Brogden's Park. Having a joint
sale with an M.P., and such an eminent auctioneer
to dispose of the animals, made me think at the
time no less of my own judgment, nor any more of
the judgment of experienced breeders.   At last the
animals were selected to be retained, which consisted of the most fashionable portion of my herd,
not omitting the three red calves previously purchased. The selection for sale included the Blanches,
and all others gathered up of local reputation, and
their produce, imagining they were almost valueless
to breed from, as Mr. Fashion now ruled with a
pretty high hand, and according to his taste nothing
must be retained but the very best.   At last the
fatal time arrived, the day was bright and cheery,
the assembly of more than an ordinary nature, but
the cattle bred by myself were scarcely in accordance
with the company for want of experience, yet
Blanche Rose 3rd, a heifer bred by Mr. Cheney,
leaving 44gs. for a few months keep, did not
speak badly for my judgment in purchasing, three
cheers were given for the young shorthorn breeder
as she changed owners, at the sum of 100gs.,
Blossom, another of the same prolific and robust
family realized 65gs., after breeding two bull calves,
which I sold when about four months old for 27gs.,
and 20gs. respectively, her cost price being 40gs.,
as she was one of the three original purchases at that
sum, any other animal in the sale with good looks,

especially those that were aiming in the direction of fashion, realized satisfactory figures, and a general average of £46 was not then to be despised by a late inexperienced breeder.

> Fashion, it is true, gained the day,
> Prudence and Perseverance aided on the way;
> I was glad the exam' was o'er at last,
> Hand joined in hand, or I would not have passed.

M

CHAPTER V.

PURCHASING BY FASHION, AND SELLING BY FASHION
TO THE INEXPERIENCED, PURCHASING A DUKE,
PURCHASING THE REMNANT OF MR. HARVEY'S
HERD, THE LOSS BY PURITY THROUGH INBREEDING,
AND BEING PREJUDICED. SATISFACTORY RESULTS
IN THE SALE OF 1875, OR IN OTHER WORDS, PASSING
THE FINAL EXAMINATION AS A SHORTHORN BREEDER.

One difficulty after another appears to the writer
to be got over in shorthorn breeding as easily as in
many other things we have to contend with as we
pass through life, but as soon as we are free from
one, another frequently makes its appearance; so it
was with me after having a successful sale and
satisfactory examination; the question was then, what
am I to do next? to obey Fashion's demands, to
move on with the times of 1873, or to stand still, as
Prejudice might advise, or even more, go back to
the time I have spoken of in 1846.   Surely none of
my readers would wish me to travel back with my
ideas, but rather move steadily on with the improve-
ments of the present age, as I was most anxious to
do in shorthorn breeding; but it was a hard battle
to fight, having so many advisers buzzing in one's

ears. So at last I made up my mind to take my own course, and have not only good animals but good pedigrees too, as I found to meet the rising market I must throw away the old-fashioned notion of prejudice, that we must not depart from what our fathers did before us; so I determined to strike out a course of my own, and to pursue it from the foundation, but experience said don't travel at too great a speed for fear of danger, but persevere on the line of Prudence to accomplish your object. I well remember travelling in the month of July, in the same year, into Gloucestershire, when Mr. Fashion was my companion to the sale, where I bent my steps, with the intent of purchasing something good; by what line I travelled I scarcely know, but at any rate, carried out the instructions of my companion to the letter, by purchasing "Cherry Duchess 13th," for 555gs., a bold stroke of business I admit, but she was truly a grand cow, and in calf to " Oxford Beau," a very fine animal indeed; the result of this union proved to be a magnificent bull, which an inexperienced breeder, came from some distance to buy, he admitted he liked the calf, but said he simply wanted him to cross ordinary dairy cattle; he also explained to me that he did not care for shorthorns at all, as he thought they were not up to much; I asked him as politely as I could under the circumstances, where would he get his good bulls from, to cross his ordinary cattle with, if there were

not some foolish people like myself to breed the
females; his reply was, he had never given that a
thought, but he did not forget to leave a cheque for
250gs. for the first calf from Cherry Duchess 13th,
and shortly after another, the right side of a 1,000gs.,
for a pair of cows that cost me less than half
that sum, besides leaving their produce behind
them, which realized nearly the same amount; this
is not a difficult lesson of experience to remember,
even if my memory is not quite so good as it was in
times past.   Just think for one moment such a
person commencing to breed shorthorns; was it because he had fallen in love with them, or what other
reason could he give after his previous explanation?
that he did not admire them; at any rate, I am certain
the animals he purchased from me were up to perfection in one point, and that was in their price.
I am afraid he can give no other reason for his purchasing than to please Mr. Fashion, as he has great
persuasive powers, he is a dangerous master, but a
good servant; he may be a pleasant companion, but
a costly one; if he is not kept under subjection,
while he remains under the protection of Prudence
and Experience, his services are invaluable; but left
to himself to advise an inexperienced youth in his
purchases, might be as far out of it as the man who
spent 1,000gs. for two animals that he believed
were not up to much until he went into partnership
with his friend Fashion.

Another winter had now nearly passed away, and the sale season commenced rather earlier than usual; the first took place in North Lancashire, which I attended of course, to see if anything fashionable could be picked up worth the money, when I stood quietly looking on, and gave but a single bid, to my astonishment, the animal fell to my lot, and I thought him rather cheap, as he carried with him the title of Grand Duke; he cost me but a little over 200gs., when I knew him to be worth much more; 300gs. was readily offered, but in vain; 320 was the next temptation, but it did not suffice; at the end of a fortnight 400gs. was proposed and accepted; the animal was then despatched to his new quarters, which left me once more in a difficulty in being without a sire; so there was no other way but travelling again in search of one, as I really must have a good male with a good pedigree in my herd; Mr. Fashion whispered by a Duke, so a Duke I bought, which my readers will think was dearly bought too, when they read that his price was 1,200gs.; it certainly was a risky piece of business for a tenant farmer to transact, and a high price to give; the principal question to answer, I suppose, will be, did he pay? Yes! he paid his price within a hair's breadth in fees for services; but what did he not do more? he gave my herd a name that did not end within a small radius of a few miles. No! the sound travelled across the Atlantic, where men of

enterprise have travelled before, and will undoubtedly travel again.   I will put the question
once more, was I right or wrong, when I purchased
one of the last sons of the memorable 7th Duke of
York?   Am I not fairly entitled to answer I was
right when I purchased 2nd Duke of Gloucester
(28392) for that was his name, and that of his lovely
dam, 11th Duchess of Geneva, he was a sire with a
constitution like iron, he had a head that every
experienced breeder could not but admire, his loins
were full and wide, flank deep, and thighs heavy, his
calves were full of gaiety and hair, there was no mis-
taking them to be the sons and daughters of a
" Duke."

> For years he stood as a noble sire,
> For followers of Bates to admire.

I must not dwell longer upon the admiration of
my old favourite, as the year 1874 is one of
importance in my history, and must relate how I
spent a second 1,200gs. the same spring in shorthorns.   A large proportion of my readers will have
read, or heard of the late Mr. Harvey, Walton-upon-
the-Hill, near Liverpool ; few better judges, I may
add better breeders, than the late Mr. Harvey in his
day, it was not a mere fancy, or hobby, to breed
shorthorns, but he was a strict admirer of purity of
blood, and clung to it, until the writer bought the
remnant of his herd, which consisted of six animals
of the Lally branch of Barringtons, it is somewhat

doubtful whether we have even now a branch of cattle that are more fruitful, where prejudice allied with fashion has not been strictly adhered to. My purchases differed a little in their breeding but not in name, three of the animals were what was termed pure, having no cross of any other blood since they had passed from the hands of Mr. Bates, Lally 6th, by 3rd Lord Oxford, her dam being Lally 3rd, by 4th Duke of Oxford, Lally 12th, a daughter of the 6th and by 3rd Duke of Claro and Lally Duchess 3rd, a daughter of the 12th by Grand Prince of Claro, he was a son of 2nd Duke of Claro 21516, from the pure Kirklevington 9th, these were the three animals that were strictly pure beyond the Usurer blood in the Duchesses, they were looked upon by Prejudice as more valuable than their relations, and as a rule, the writer looks upon Purists as friends of prejudice, and not friends in reality to shorthorn breeding, I do not mean by Purists, admirers of purity of blood, but persons who are prejudiced against any small infusion of pure blood, added to pedigrees by other experienced breeders equally as judiciously and as purely descended for generations, as the animals which are imagined by Prejudice and his friends, to have a superiority in money value over their companions.

Having now briefly described the breeding of half of the 1,200gs. purchase, I must next explain the other half that were not supposed to be so

valuable, which were Lally 11th, a white cow, five
years of age, her roan heifer calf, one month old, by
Grand Prince of Claro 28781, which I named Lally
Duchess 2nd, and her own sister, twelve months old
named Lally Duchess, the youngster's dam was by
Lord Wild Eyes 5th, also bred by Mr. Harvey, he
was a son of the American 3rd Lord Oxford, from Wild
Eyes 24th, by 4th Duke of Oxford, the dam of
Lally 11th, was a daughter of Duke of Wetherby,
by 7th Duke of York, from the renowned Duchess
77th, Lally 2nd, the great grand-dam of Lally
Duchess, and Lally Duchess 2nd, was by the
Canterbury Royal winner named " Malachite," a
son of Duke of Moscow, a sire with four successive
crosses of Duke Bulls; his dam was Cowslip 3rd,
by Mr. Bates's " Chieftain," grand dam by Mr.
Bates's " Duke of Norfolk," great grand dam by
" Waterloo," the sire of " Belvedere," and of the
same family as Belvedere himself, a bull that Mr.
Bates thought good enough to take two crosses in
succession upon his idolized Duchess's.   The
next generation in the Lally pedigree is " Lally,"
by " Earl of Derby."   The antecedents of both
Lally 11th and 12th here stand on an equality, as
they are both descended from Lally, it is my duty to
next point out what fault Mr. Prejudice had to find
with the breeders of such a bull as the winner at
Canterbury; firstly, he says he is not of the tribe
of Israel but a Malachite, although he has a

similarity in blood for generations past, yet he is
not descended from Israel but from the Amalachites;
secondly, look at the name of "Malachite" in a
Bates pedigree, it is an absurdity to the extreme to
think of accepting him in their society, he may be
well descended, a good animal, and improve his
produce in personal appearance upon their dams,
but we must have purity of blood. After having
the opinion of Mr. Prejudice upon the breeding of
the latter half of my 1,200gs. purchase, there
appeared but faint hopes of ever having a profitable
return, and I am afraid Mr. Fashion's opinion was
united with that of his companion; but as I named
in the early part of this chapter, I would strike out
a course of my own, independent of the companionship of Fashion and Prejudice, but with Perseverance
and Prudence, felt sure I should gain experience
how to become their master in shorthorn breeding.

I must now return to the pure branch of my latest
purchase. Lally 6th, not being in calf when I
bought her, was looked upon as rather a suspicious
character; her daughter the 12th was then all that
could be desired in a Bates shorthorn, as she had
calved Lally Duchess 3rd a few days previous to
the completion of my bargain, apparently there was
every prospect of their becoming a numerous family,
as the dam was in the prime of life and had only
just passed her fourth summer, the calf by her side

N

was a beautiful red, and full of admiration; before
many weeks had expired 250gs. had been offered in
exchange for her, but Mr. Fashion whispered no!
she is one of the purest Lallies in existence, and
must be valuable, so she still remained in my herd;
but how were her dam and grand-dam spending their
time? The latter had done nothing but eat the
food of idleness since she came into my possession,
so she was dispatched to the butcher, and her
daughter followed her bad example, as never
another living Lally was added to the herd from
her, simply a premature one, but I suppose the calf
would be pure, as it was by the 1,200gs. Duke. As
she had followed in the footsteps of her dam in life,
she was also doomed to an early death. Lally
Duchess 3rd was the only female offspring descended
from dam and grand dam, they had made a bad
use of their time, but the grand-daughter still
worse, as she gradually sickened and died, which
made me be rather doubtful if she was inwardly
pure in every point.

But let me pass on from this doleful tale to the 2nd
half that was so full of prejudice, and deficient in
fashion. Poor Lally 11th, robust, strong and a
good breeder, had to succumb to the foot and mouth
disease, in not being able to deliver her calf when
the fever was at its height; her eldest daughter was
a pretty little cow, whose descendants are flourishing

even at the present day, and her younger sister I
sold when a yearling for 500gs. to cross the Atlantic,
a most beautiful heifer, and well descended in the
estimation of the experienced buyer who purchased
her, but I understood from the critics that she was
not strictly pure; but what is the good of purity of
blood to any breeder if he does not retain the constitution and fecundity? Perseverance in breeding
is of no avail without prudence; no doubt that
every care had been taken to preserve their purity,
but little to preserve the constitution; the writer
had to reap the reward of prejudice and fashion in
loosing his 600gs. by being too closely bred by
others before him; yet he had the advantage of the
good judgment of the alliance between Malachite
and Lally, as the descendants of their daughter,
Lally 2nd, are now numerous, and to an experienced
Bates breeder, robust and fashionable; but the
descendants of Lally 3rd, her half-sister, by 4th
Duke of Oxford, is it not sad to say all that are now
remaining in England are two individuals, one a
daughter of the 500gs. Lally 15th, and the other a
grand-daughter of the 600gs. Lally 18th.

I must now move on with my history to the
autumn of 1874 when I made two more important
but unfortunate purchases in grand Duchess of
Oxford 25th and 28th, two sisters, but by different
sires, at a price of over 1,400gs.; the former was

injured, and had to be sold as a doubtful breeder; the
latter had but two calves. when she was also injured,
and had to be slaughtered, her eldest calf, a heifer,
died at eighteen days old, through the effects of
eating wheat straw before being strong enough to
digest it; is this also not a lesson of experience
worth remembering? but what made the loss more
painful, 700gs. was offered for the calf as soon as
she became well, but that day never came, so I had
to be content with receiving 200gs. for her brother,
in the place of the 700gs. for the sister, this was the
melancholy end of my breeding Oxfords. I am afraid
I am getting on slowly with the explanation of my
final examination as a fashionable shorthorn breeder,
but I have passed over in my experiences many
lessons of less importance with the exception
of profit, but have found that it is the unprofitable
ones that strike the deepest root. I had by this
time added to my herd two animals of the Waterloo
family, and a daughter of that fine old cow " Rose
of Raby " (so well known at Holker), by 6th Duke
of Airdrie, her name was " Maid of Lorn." She
bred me two heifers in succession, to which I gave
the names of Rose of Raby 2nd and 3rd, the latter
was by my favourite old sire 2nd Duke of Gloucester.
But in all my purchases no cow stood more prominent
in my estimation than Cherry Duchess 13th, her
noble carriage was sufficient to make every passer-
by notice her graceful style, even the village

blacksmith had his eyes fixed upon her for a considerable time before he could find words to express himself in his own language; at last his ideas were collected, and burst forth with the exclamation, I may take a long look at her, as I shall hardly ever see as much money walking about in a field again.

Although Cherry Duchess 13th was extremely grand, my three reds purchased as calves were equally as pretty, especially the 300gs. Kirklevington Duchess 7th, which was one of the sweetest-looking shorthorns that I ever possessed, perhaps for more reasons than her personal beauty, as she carried it out practically in breeding me two calves in a little over twelve months; that did not betray her sweetness in the prices they realized, the son, at a little over sixteen months old, made 110gs., and was thought good enough to travel beyond the Atlantic, a space of 3,000 miles; his tiny sister had been only born 14 weeks when she did not disgrace herself by scampering round the ring at Conishead sale in 1875, until she changed owners at 360gs., when her dam, a few minutes previously, not allowing the last saud to run from Mr. Thornton's glass before she reached 660gs. Now I must ask you who are prejudiced to refer back to 1872 when the 300gs. calf was doomed to never pay. Allow me to return one moment to her breeding, as it was her good breeding as well as her good looks that made her

sell, and I feel sure that my readers will agree
with me, that a word of advice from an experienced
breeder is worth remembering, when I tell them
that this is a grand-daughter of Kirklevington 10th,
by Delhi, that Mr. Bell pronounced the best of her
family up to that number, Kirklevington Duchess
7th, was by Duke of Kirklevington (25982), a son of
7th Duke of York, her dam Kirklevington 18th by 3rd
Lord Oxford, a grand cow in her day, often admired,
as well as coveted, she had the honour of turning a
great man away in a rage by being refused to become his property. I must not forget to name
Kirklevington 24th, her companion and relative, as she
was also a grand-daughter of Kirklevington 10th, but
by 5th Duke of Wharfdale, from Kirklevington 17th,
by Lord Lally; this was the 100gs. calf that I had
also bought four years previously by the advice of
Mr. Bell, she too bred for me a son and a daughter,
the son was sold at six months old for 60gs.; his
sister, Kirklevington 26th, at the same age, made
390gs., to travel to Canada; and her dam 420gs. to
remain in England. Lady Barrington 9th, the 77gs.
calf, also bred a son and a daughter in the same
period; the son met with a premature death to the
butcher, but his sister made up for the loss in selling for 265gs. as a yearling, and her dam the same
day realizing 360gs. I might as well add another
to the trio of purchases in calves, that makes
the business look more four square in com-

pletion ; she was one of the Wild Eyes tribe, that
came into my possession a little after the other
three, and did not idle her time when in my
hands, as her cost price was but 50gs, realizing
255gs. at the same time as the others, for California;
and her heifer calf 160gs., for Canada. Having now
mixed the sweet, with the bitter, sufficiently for
any young breeder to get a glimpse of the results of
fashionable shorthorn breeding, by my experience
given in this chapter, I must now draw it to a close
by winding up with showing how I became, not
only a fashionable but a practical shorthorn breeder,
which year was equally as important to me as
the one that had passed before it, as I well knew
that I had to pass the final examination before
another had set in ; the dreaded day appeared
to draw closer and closer; but as I had very quickly
found by experience that there was nothing equal to
perseverance with prudence, to overcome the greatest
difficulty, I had made up my mind to overcome them
all by their aid, on the 14th day of September.
After the expensive lessons received from Mr.
Fashion since I left the village school, I gained
confidence that I would be able to answer all
questions put before me by Inspector Thornton, at
Conishead Priory, where he would attend ; so at
last the final day arrived, when scrutineers were
both numerous and select, which caused me to find
that no half measures would be passed, but a

thorough examination, not in theory, but practically
would have to be gone through before that day had
passed away; naturally I felt a little nervous for
fear all should not be in my favour, but the inspector
bid me to be of good cheer, that he carried within
his breast a vocabulary that would explain the
deepest mystery before the bright sun had set, and
without giving any further time, called out for
question number one to be answered immediately.
Perhaps my readers would wish me to explain in
figures

What he did for me in the days of old,
It is as pleasant a tale as ever was told ;
Both Conishead and cattle were much admired,
The company, all that could be desired.

The good old " Maid of Lorn " led off the Ball,
At one hundred and fifteen Thornton let the hammer fall ;
At eventide two hundred and twenty-three guineas each was
  proclaimed,
Even so, the writer passed his final as a shorthorn breeder
  famed.

CHAPTER VI.

TABLE OF FIGURES, THE REASON THE ANIMALS VARIED IN THEIR PRICES, PURCHASING LARGELY FOR CANADA PRINCIPALLY THROUGH FASHION AND PREJUDICE, TOO CLOSE BREEDING, INJURIOUS, COM· PARING SHORTHORN BREEDING TO A MANUFACTORY, DIFFERENT DEGREES OF FASHION.

After passing through the examination so triumphantly on the 14th of September, by placing the larger half of my herd in the hands of the public, and their realisation being fully 40gs. each more than I anticipated, is a proof that neither fashion, nor prejudice, had led me beyond their money value in purchasing them or their ancestors; but as I am now writing upon experience in short-horn breeding, by request, I have a desire that every point should be made clear to my readers, and give them sufficient evidence of my testimony, by placing a table before them in figures (and the writer has found by experience that figures are very truthful things), giving the cost price of every animal bought, the time when purchased, and what they realized with their produce, leaving it to the discretion of the admirers of shorthorns, deductions to be made for keep, and interest of money laid out.

o

Table of Prices of Animals sold on the 14th September, 1875, by John Thornton, at Coniskead Priory, giving the Cost Price of every Animal, and Date of Purchase, and what they realized with their Produce.

Name of Animal.	Date of Produce.	Cost Price.	At what sold.	Sale of Produce.	Total Realization.
		Gs.	Gs.	Gs.	Gs.
Maid of Lorn ..	October, 1873	210	115	320	435
Wildeyes Gwynne 2nd	July, 1875	60	74	..	74
Lady Waterloo 18th	May, 1874	120	150	..	150
Double Gwynne	October, 1870	28	235	212	447
Lady Barrington 9th	March, 1871	77	360	282	642
Kirkleyton 24th	July, 1871	100	420	450	870
Wild Eyes 31st	May, 1872	50	265	100	415
Daine Gwynne	October, 1872	81	125	15	150
Kirkleyton Duchess 7th	April, 1872	300	660	470	1130
Cherry Oxford 2nd	Calved February, 1873	..	200	..	200
Butteroup 21st	Calved March, 1873	..	41	..	41
Lady Waterloo 26th	July, 1873	105	280	..	280
Lally Duchess 2nd	March, 1874	100	500	..	500
Cameo 8th	May, 1875	50	75	..	75
Oxford Minstrel	July, 1875	60	93	..	93
Minstrel 6th	May, 1875	100	175	..	175
Master Wildeyes	March, 1875	25	135	..	185
		1466	3893	1909	5812 — sum realized
					1466 — cost price
					4356 — difference

It will be taken as a special favour, if my readers
will glance carefully over the table of figures placed
before them, and notice in particular dates of purchases, to what family each purchase belongs, as
well as the difference in their results. Taking for
instance the only heifers sold that were over two
years of age of my own breeding, and only a few days
difference in their birth, but mark the difference in
price, Buttercup 21st, the last of the family that I
commenced to breed from in 1860, only realized
41gs., being in calf; while her companion in life,
Cherry Oxford 2nd, descended from Cherry by
Pirate (2430), made 200gs.; they were both fed
exactly on the same food, and grazed in the same
field, but not bred in the same way; the former,
for want of experience; the latter, by the benefit of
it. I will next take "Double Gwynne," which
name she derives from her sire, as well as her dam,
being of one family, which was also the principal
reason of her realizing 235gs.; while "Dame
Gwynne," from the same place, but carelessly
bred, sold on the same day for 125gs., and in many
respects her equal as an animal; but Wildeyes
Gwynne 2nd, bred by the same gentleman,
was not equal to either in one way or another, as
she only made 74gs., through being so much
jumbled up in her breeding, that she was neither
good for an admirer, of Bates, Booth, or a Gwynne.
While "Double Gwynne" was sold to me through

Prejudice at a lower price, for the only reason that
she was not by a Booth bull, but by a " Gwynne,"
and that was the very reason I purchased her and
left the other two behind me.   I will next take two
of the Minstrel branch of the Gwynnes, named
"Oxford Minstrel 2nd, and "Minstrel 6th," both by
Bates bulls, and descended from same grand-dam
" Minstrel 4th," which had two daughters in experienced hands that made over 500gs. each, while
the former of the two animals that I have named
realized but 93gs., through the injudicious cross of a
Booth bull, admitted by an inexperienced breeder ;
the latter animal mentioned contained but the half-
cross of the same blood, sold for 175gs.   I have
alluded to the breeding sufficiently to show why the
prices of some of the animals were so far below the
other ; it was not personal merit alone that made
the difference in their value, but either judicious or
injudicious crosses, added by experienced or inexperienced hands, as well as the difference in the
popularity of the tribes; but the Kirklevingtons and
Barringtons stood then, as they stand now, much
admired, often coveted, but not always to be
obtained.   It is entirely at our own discretion
whether we breed fashionable, or unfashionable
animals ; but it is not prudent to be prejudiced,
either for one or the other, beyond what is profitable.

After the disposal of the animals before mentioned, I still retained my favourite old bull, 5 Lallies, 2 Oxfords, and a Kirklevington, besides a few others, some of which, fashion did not admit into their society. Never was it more true that they came from the East and the West, the North and the South, as it was on the 14th day of September, as visitors not only appeared, but purchased for California, Canada and Nova Scotia. After this remarkable event in my career, as a breeder, I was invited to purchase animals for Canada of the most fashionable and costly nature, to lay the foundation of an extensive herd, which my employer informed me he had a desire for it to be, not only the largest, but the most fashionable in that country, and to accomplish that object I had not to spare my hand in placing it deep into his pocket; but with all these privileges, the work was difficult to perform, as I soon found I could not oblige him in his ambition with a satisfactory result, as it was frequently compulsory on my part to act injudiciously in purchasing animals to some extent to oblige prejudice, which was undoubtedly an hindrance to make the work a success, as I had to fight strongly against prejudice, combined with fashion, and they are certainly two dangerous opponents to contend with. If I had only been allowed the privilege of acting through Prudence and Perseverance by the advice of Experience they would easily have been conquered;

but when bound to Fashion through Prejudice,
against experience, the task is most difficult to
accomplish, as instructions were given me by
Prejudice, to purchase for Fashion certain animals
at any cost, leaving Prudence and Experience in
the back ground. To lay the foundation of an
extensive and fashionable herd like this, with a view
to paying a reasonable per centage, does not require
going at it with a rush, like a train entering in at
one end of a tunnel and out at the other, but quite
the reverse, if the purchaser intends to become a
shorthorn breeder of note or permanent standing,
compulsory measures are of no avail in either buying or breeding, but prudence must have her own
time and way, and not be compelled to breed in and
in for ever, or to purchase indiscreetly to oblige
either Prejudice or Fashion.

I trust my readers will not think me too severe
upon inbreeding, as I am really fond of it, to a
certain extent, to keep up type and uniformity; but
saw the evil of indulging in it too deeply thirty
years ago, still at no more distant date than
twenty years, when I beheld animal after animal
pine away for reasons unknown to many ; but the
writer knew it then, and knows it still, even less
than ten years have elapsed since he saw the disease
nearer and nearer, it was hovering round about his
own herd, and at last it called upon him and took

away animals full of aristocratic blood, costly purchases, without leaving a profitable return. And
why is all this? Simply high feeding, and injudicious breeding, from one generation to another;
had the writer not experienced it, he would not have
written it. The Americans laid the temptation for
us, in asking for pure or line bred animals; we
went in search and found them out; the prices went
up for purity of blood, but down for constitution,
and shorthorn breeding; purity of pedigree was all
that was then required, animal or no animal, when
the fever was raging; but they, like ourselves, are
beginning to get their eyes opened, and require to
look at the animal before taking it across the
Atlantic. Some of the present branches they
sought after, where are they now? They are
scarcely here, or there, but almost extinct; take
for example, the Fuschia tribe once so popular, and
I may add once so pretty, there are now but half-
a-dozen animals remaining in England of this
family that were considered pure enough to please
the most fashionable breeder, and only one has been
exported for years past. What have become of the
animals of this inbred tribe? They have gradually
worn out like an inebriate man, before half the time
of his natural life is expired. Only a few years
have elapsed since this was one of the most admired
families of Bates cattle in England, and when they
left Captain Blathwayt's, in Gloucestershire, for Lord

Dunmore's, in Scotland, in the year 1874, at a cost of over 400gs. each, they were as hardy and as pretty a lot of animals as eye would desire to look upon. The piercing winds of Scotland appeared to be too much for their refinement, but from the sale at Dunmore, in 1875, they travelled back to the extreme South of England, at a more costly price than the original one. In their new home they fared sumptuously every day, principally upon artificial food, more than was natural to any breeding animal, to hold the constitution together, and to some extent the removal into the Northern climate, and followed by excessive living in the South, did equally as much harm to break up the constitution of this family as the inbreeding had done, but still when I allow sufficiently on climate and injudicious feeding, why should they have disappeared as a tribe any more than the Fantails, another branch from the same foundation which are still numerous, prolific, and robust, and equally as well bred, providing Mr. Prejudice keeps aloof, as he is almost sure to condemn the breeding of the late Sir Charles Knightley's Touchstone and Barleycorn, which blood they carry within their veins, and no doubt to some extent have been the means of preserving this branch of the family. The Fidgets, a third offshoot from Fletcher by a son of Young Wynyard are numerous where new blood has been added, but from Fidget 7th, by 3rd Lord Oxford, there is but one daughter and her offspring to uphold the purity in England, which have all now passed into the hands of Mr. Ellis, of Summersbury Hall, in Surrey.

The seekers of pure or what is termed line bred animals, raise them to a fabulous price, and tempt many a young and inexperienced breeder in a wrong direction towards improving his herd even in the present day, as the writer knows full well the temptation offered by Fashion, to be resisted when business is brisk, it is not shorthorn breeding alone that he depends on then, it is in making wise purchases and profitable sales where the benefit lies, it is not always the manufacturer that receives the most profit from his goods, but the shrewd man of business, who follows after him. By the experience that I have gained in shorthorns I would advise any young man to be a manufacturer in preference to the other, providing he builds his factory upon a good foundation, as that is the chief point in the commencement of breeding, but it is not all, as after the factory is built, it requires machinery to work it, and after the machinery is purchased, it requires the knowledge of managing the machinery, and without that knowledge both the machinery and the factory are useless, however valuable the foundation may be when first laid. Have I not shown in my previous chapters what I and my father did in shorthorn breeding in our youth, by

P

throwing down what others had carefully built up, each of us had a good foundation to build upon, but for want of experience could not carry out the building of a herd that others had commenced before us, no! it requires time and experience to become a manufacturer, even if it be only for a herd of shorthorns, no matter whether it is a herd of extreme fashion, or one entirely free from it, but we must in our breeding prepare for sale what the market requires, and undoubtedly they must be such animals to meet that requirement as the present fashion demands, some may ask what is the present fashion, the best answer that I can give, let every one breed according to his own taste, but not to forget that in winning a race only one obtains the prize, but frequently many are highly commended, and to all who attain that honour I would say be content, as one has his mind bent upon winning the Champion prize at the Royal, another at the Christmas Fat Show, both are equally right in their own way, and according to their own taste, a third is content if he gains the highest honours at a County Show, his companion rests satisfied with surpassing his neighbours at a local one, there is a wide contrast between the first and the last I have named, but the last is equal in his ambition to the first, to gain the chief honours in that Society in which he competes, whether he produces an animal for the Royal, Smithfield, the British Dairy Show, or the sale ring, his ambition is equally as great in trying to surpass the other competitors. As regards fashion, the winner at Smithfield is fashionable there, but not as a breeding shorthorn; the champion at the Dairy Show is fashionable there, but it may not be so, if in company with the Royal visitor; reversing the case, and placing the Royal winner at the Dairy Show, I am afraid that out of its own society it will not be fashionable, and it might be that the most fashionable animal in a sale ring would not be a fit companion for any of the other three; but why is this so? Firstly, the animal at the Royal is too frequently so excessively fat, that rarely we hear of its offspring following its example; as a rule the Smithfield champion is beyond hope as a breeder, and the Dairy winner too often as far behind in appearance to a fashionable bred shorthorn as a dairymaid is to a Duchess. I hope I have clearly shown what is fashionable for one purpose is not for another, and what is fashionable to one breeder is not to another; fashionably bred animals have different degrees in fashion, and for different purposes.

Firstly, I will refer to a nobleman, on his breeding establishment, all must be of the highest class there, without considering the cost of its production, as well as being fashionable to the highest degree. If he makes up his mind to purchase the best of everything, he has it in his power to do it. Secondly, the Squire may also be fond of fashionable blood, yet his ambition rarely leads him on to be a rival with the noble Lord ; and lastly, the small landowner or the tenant farmer is equally as ambitious in his own sphere of life, but experience teaches him that he must not travel beyond his depth on the same line of fashion as the other two, but breed from such animals as Prudence will admit to be the best and most fashionable, adapted for his position in life, and the land he occupies. Fashion has often changed, and will undoubtedly often change again ; yet there have been different degrees of fashion for centuries back, and there will be different degrees to the end of time ; and a continual warfare will remain between her and Prejudice, as bitter as it has ever existed for many a long year before any date that the writer can give upon his experience in shorthorns.

CHAPTER VII.

FASHION AND PRICES AT THEIR HEIGHT, SIGNS
OF THEIR DECLINE, PROFITABLE PURCHASES,
DIFFERENCE BETWEEN THE AMERICANS AND
AUSTRALIANS, WHY MR. BATES USED CLEVELAND
LAD (3408), THE SCHOOL OF EXPERIENCE.

A year had now passed away since the day of
that most remarkable event that ever took place in
my shorthorn history, the close of 1876 was near at
hand, and I had explained but little of my doings
for that season, beyond the extensive purchases
that 1 made for Canada, which will ever be remembered as a mark in my experience upon shorthorns, it was a year that I think can claim the very
height of fashion above all others, and not only the
height in that respect, but in prices too, as 1,600gs.
had to be paid for a pair of Kirklevingtons before
they could be obtained, and even then, to be had
only as a special favour; and 1,000gs. for a pair of
the best of Gwynne's appears a ridiculous sum to
give, when now they can be had for 100gs.; 1,000gs.
had to be remitted before the best and purest of the
Wild Eyes was allowed to leave her native home;
1,700gs. was offered, but rejected, for an Oxford
heifer calf; 2,500gs. had to be paid for one of

England's best of that family, and the same sum
for a Noble Duke, and truly he was deserving of his
name, as he stood in the position of Champion in
the show ring, and one of the best of sires ever
since he crossed the Atlantic, his price was then
and is still, the highest of any male, that ever left
England's shores, even if it had been double the
amount it would never have been regretted being
paid by the owner of the 4th Duke of Clarence
(33596), as he was then one of England's choice,
and remains even now, in his 14th year, to be one
of Canada's best.

Am I not right when I say prices ruled high in
1876 for fashionable animals, as the writer, after
the completion of his Canadian purchases, secured
one of our purest English Princesses at 360gs,
which left him 100gs. profit at the end of a single
week? Is this not a lesson of profit, what he
previously stated, that the merchant frequently
obtained by his merchandise, a larger percentage than
the manufacturer? But it is to the latter that he
more especially wishes to refer. If the breeder is a
man of experience in his undertaking, he can readily
dispose of his merchandise, according to the value
of his manufactured article, especially when made
of the best quality. I am afraid that I am wander-
ing away a little too far from my experience, by
comparing shorthorn breeding to a manufacturer,

to please the majority of my readers; so I suppose my pen must scribble along respecting the doings amongst cattle alone, and leave behind me the imagination of tall chimneys.

As I was just thinking of settling down for the winter after my tour through England in search of shorthorns for Canada, when I found that a good Barrington could scarcely be bought for money, and that a Duchess was not available at a price prudent to pay, I unexpectedly had the offer of two Wild Eyes cows, in calf, and two yearling heifers, that I ultimately purchased for 1,600gs., which closed my shorthorn labours for the season. When another year had commenced, men began to whisper one to another that the shorthorn fever was abating, and all would soon be well, except in cases where the parties had purchased largely when it was at its height, so surely I was in for the disease as the fever had not left me, which made me begin to think what would be the best means to get rid of the complaint, so I consulted the physician in London, that I had applied to before, and he advised that I should invite my friends together, and see if they could not assist me by their means to release me of this malady, which had entirely now fallen into my pocket; of course, I must not pay a physician and not take his advice; so I at last invited my friends to meet him at Conishead Grange,

on the 6th day of September, 1877, when a general
consultation took place; but after the consultation,
an operation had to be performed, which resulted in
a perfect cure by one of the Wild Eyes cows I had
recently purchased, one yearling heifer, and the two
newly-born calves realizing the sum of 2,058gs.,
leaving in my possession one cow and one of the
heifers, which were both in calf, being worth at that
time, at a reasonable estimate, 1,000gs., which would
be in addition to the 2,058gs already received,
making a total of 3,058gs. for 1,600gs. outlay
over a period of ten months; this is surely worth
recording in my experience upon shorthorns, and
certainly a lesson that I should very much like to
have often repeated, as a general average of £153
for twenty-seven head was as much as could be
expected, when the sale included, three doubtful
breeders that had wearied my patience in endeavour-
ing to get them to be remunerative, their persistency
obliged me to give them up, although fashionable.
These were the only non-breeders that I had been
troubled with since my commencement of keeping
highly-bred animals; their names were "Cherry
Duchess 13th," "Lally 12th," and "Grand Duchess
of Oxford 25th." This was one of the three Northern
sales that was named at the time, in the Agricultural
journals, as being full of interest.   Mr. Staniforth's,
of "Storrs Hall," and Mr. Cochrane's animals being
removed from Canada to Windermere to be disposed

of, were the other two; the last named included two
of the "Airdrie Duchesses, viz:—3rd Duchess of
Hillhurst and 5th Duchess of Hillhurst, the former
purchased by Mr. Loder, of Whittlebury, for the
sum of 4,100gs., and the latter by Lord Bective at
4,300gs., Mr. Longman taking 2nd Duke of Hillhurst in exchange for 800gs., at six years old; such
prices as the two yearlings realized are unparalleled
in England, with the exception of Duke of Connaught
bought by Lord Fitzhardinge, in Lord Dunmore's
sale in 1875, for 4,500gs., the general average for forty
head at Mr. Cochrane's sale was £197 not including
either Duke or Duchesses, Mr. Stainforth's thirty-
nine head of Booth cattle made 85gs. each, of the
animals included in the Conishead, twenty-seven
head, nine were calves, or under twelve months old.

I still retained in my herd the Lally, Wild Eyes,
Kirklevington, Oxford, and Fuschia families, quite
sufficient in both numbers and quality to make a
first-class herd of shorthorns. After this profitable
sale I became a little more cautious in not launching
out too deeply in purchasing, as things appeared a
little darker for investments of that description, but
picked up old cows or heifers with some little
change of blood in their pedigree, at a lower figure
than was palatable to the purists, as I had found
by experience the danger of too close breeding,
especially in old families, altho' the Americans

Q

were as keen as ever over the line bred animals as they termed them, and could not be persuaded that the constitution of some of them was on a sliding scale towards ruin.　Animals with four successive crosses of Duchess blood upon old pedigrees were eagerly sought after, when pure pedigrees throughout could not be obtained, or even animals with only five successive crosses of either pure Bates or Booth blood, descended from a dairy cow, in preference to any good blood that was not line bred from the foundation.　About a year previous to this time, I was invited to purchase four females for Australia, at a price of 500gs. each, the animals had to be well formed, with not less than four direct crosses of pure Bates blood, last added to an old pedigree, but not necessarily to be what was termed a Bates pedigree, but their last four crosses being strictly pure, were considered of more importance than the original portion of the pedigree, yet the animals had to descend from the blood of breeders half a century back, here the Australians differed in their opinions to the Americans, ten years ago, as five direct crosses of pure Bates blood, even if the sixth cross was an Aberdeen Angus, satisfied them, they even went so far as to think the Angus would do less injury to a pedigree, (but perhaps not the animal), than a sixth cross of shorthorn blood, if it was not in direct descent with the other five, but how long did this last, quite as long as any experienced breeder could expect it to

have done. I remember seeing one animal sold for
300gs. by auction, only the fifth cross removed from
a dunn'd scotch cow, yet she was considered pure.
A well known and reliable breeder not far from
where the writer is using his pen, recently told him he
had known the original black colour return in the
seventh cross of shorthorn blood, and the produce
from that cross had every appearance of a true bred
shorthorn ; this shows us that old pedigrees are
much more to be relied upon than purity of short
descent, some may turn round upon me by saying
why did Mr. Bates use Cleveland Lad upon his
Duchesses? for two reasons, the first, that he contained
a large proportion of the same blood, through Young
Wynyard (2859) and Short Tail (2621), by using
Belvedere in his herd intermingled with Matchem
(2281), full of Mason and Colling blood, tracing to
Hubback (319), the bull we understand, Mr. Bates
almost worshipped as an " Idol " in shorthorns, but
give the old breeder his due, he generally knew in
what direction he intended to aim with his ideas,
no doubt he had watched carefully the breeding of
Mr. Brown's Matchem cow, before he disclosed it
to others, and feeling certain that her ancestors
traced back far beyond Young Wynyard, he secured
in her what he had been eagerly looking for, to breed
a bull that would suit his purpose for the much
needed change in his Duchesses.   Secondly, Mr.
Bates had not the opportunity of obtaining so easily

as what he could have done had he been living at
the present day, the blood he required for the
alliance.   On the other hand some might remark
that prejudice held him too fast to his own opinions
to obtain it, but the writer certainly agrees with him
that his admixture was right for the Duchesses, as
experience has taught him that an abrupt alliance is
ruinous to the type, and too often to the constitution.
He remembers well an old breeder who bred his
animals so closely that he was at a standstill, at
least his cattle were, if not more, they were going back
by taking a downward course, it is certainly the
wrong way to travel before retiring from his
pursuit.   What did this old breeder do next but the
very same thing as Mr. Bates did with Cleveland
Lad, he used a bull with only four registered crosses,
which he had no doubt of being purely bred for
generations beyond the registration, as his grand-
dam was a successful winner in her day at the local
shows, undoubtedly this breeder that I am now
speaking of, had been watching her career so closely
that he was tempted to purchase her daughter, by
his own bull, and in due time she was also put to
one of his own inbred bulls, and produced a short-
legged, thick fleshed animal, which he used as a
sire to a portion of his herd, with the greatest success,
as the progeny improved in size, flesh and constitution,
but if anything destroyed their original neatness,
in returning to his inbred bulls on this animal's

produce, they gradually regained the original type,
without losing their robustness. After some years
he tried an abrupt cross with a pure Bates bull
upon a pedigree that was quite the opposite
in breeding, which resulted in entirely destroying
the type and not improving the constitution, if my
readers look upon this as correct, it certainly is
necessary for every breeder to be careful in the sires he
uses upon any kind of stock, as it requires different
characters in the male animal to suit the different
characters in the female.

Just imagine an inexperienced breeder purchasing
a bull for the only reason that he has won at the
Royal, thinking that he cannot be wrong in being
directed by the decision of the judges, no doubt the
male winner is adapted for many kinds of stock, but
it remains nothing less than a lottery to him whether
it is adapted for his own herd or not, it is only the
man of experience that discerns the difference in the
character of the male to answer his purpose, he knows
full well what will answer in one case will not answer
in another, but a weak head in a sire he certainly
will not admit in any case, and a narrow chest will
be more disgusting to him still. The writer has
also found by the little experience that he has gained
that a sire without a deep chest and flank, heavy
thighs and masculine head, is not suitable for any
breed or type, even if his beautiful level back and

neat shoulders have gained for him a distinction of
honour, or more than that, if his ancestory trace
down to the renowned Hubback, through blood of
the most fashionable and most pure up to the year
1887, it being just a century since that Shorthorn
Chief was purchased by Messrs. R. Colling and Mr.
Waistell.   Some of my readers may be induced to
think that I do not approve of pedigrees of short
descent, they that are under that impression, are
greatly mistaken, as I am most fond of trying to
improve upon the dairy cow and have frequently
purchased animals with one or two registered crosses,
then is the time for observing the good effect of a
purely bred sire, and no doubt with line breeding
soon can obtain a uniform character, but it is doubtful whether it is wise to rely too much upon their
male offspring, unless they are in want of a little
change to an inbred herd, or that the breeder knows
something of their origin before the first registered
cross, as the male is undoubtedly the animal that
has the greatest influence either for good or for harm
in their progeny.

I can well imagine a youth, in glancing over
these pages, asking himself the question who is the
writer of this rambling story, that he should dictate
to me how to breed cattle, have I not been to Cambridge University where all was to be seen and learned
that was most fashionable, and it is not more than a

few months since I left the Agricultural College, what more do I require in the knowledge of Agriculture. I very much doubt if the writer has ever taken a single lesson within these walls. It is true that he has not had that golden opportunity, but has spent half a century in a still more extensive school, where lessons are still more costly than either at the University or the Agricultural College, neither he nor any other youth can understand cattle breeding in all its branches, until he has taken a degree higher than either the University or the Agricultural College can teach, and that must be taken at the school of Experience, where' practical knowledge is gained and theoretical teaching unknown. May I not repeat the same question, who is the writer of this voluminous epistle, no other answer can be given than he is still but a scholar in that school where he will remain until his natural term of years are expired, in the hopes of gaining knowledge from the hand of Experience.

which was readily disposed of at 250gs. An exceedingly grand cow of the Craggs family cost me 150gs., which I thought at the time not too dear, she too was despatched into other hands without entering my herd, Dowager Duchess 7th and Duchess Nancy 2nd, were also obtained at 70gs. each, they were thought by others to be a great bargain, and apparently I imagined so too, as 50gs. profit was offered upon the pair before my return home, but being a little short sighted could not see to accept it, although a calf from one of them realized 63gs. the following year prevented me from taking any harm, a Barrington calf, four months old, sold for 105gs. to Mr. Jefferson, so up to the present, shorthorn breeding paid, if fashionable in their pedigree and fairly good animals.

On the 15th of May, the day following Lord Penrhyn's sale, the entire herd of fifty-two head of Bates shorthorns, the property of Mr. Larking, in Sussex, were disposed of by Mr. Stafford, a man as earnest in his work for Bates blood as the late Mr. Disraeli when Premier of England. No more reliable man than Mr. Strafford has lived since the days of Mr. Bates, not only as a shorthorn auctioneer, but in giving genuine advice upon his experience of Bates blood, but what was he doing for Mr. Larking on the day we have just named, but fighting manfully for his cause by setting the battle in array between England and Australia for the red,

R

white, and roan, which commenced by fierce action
in forcing Mr. Allsopp to pay 250gs. for the first
Siddington that Mr. Bowley ever bred at fourteen
years of age, it is true she was a magnificent animal,
but her price was not behind in grandeur, she was
by 4th Duke of Oxford, from Kirklevington 7th, by
Earl of Derby, bred by Mr. Bates.   I also imagined
with the rest of the company that it would not do
to be behind in defending England against Australia,
so opposed Mr. McCallock for Fuschia 10th and
secured her at 240gs., at nine years of age, she was
a lovely cow, with a true shorthorn character, no
animals in the sale were to be compared with this
family in uniformity.   Lady Worcester 6th, bred by
Mr. Harward, fell to the bid of Mr. Loder at 275gs.,
she too was a grand cow, Specimen 2nd, of the
Charmer family, was secured for Australia at 92gs.,
the latter had now begun in earnest as there was a
struggle between Australia and the little County of
Westmorland for Gazelle 26th, when the auctioneer
declared Australia had won the battle, but not without paying dearly for it, as the price was 425gs.,
the highest price on record for that family ; the next
stroke of business done was to decide the ownership
of Kirklevington Duchess 9th, a grand-daughter of
Kirklevington 14th, own sister to Siddington, she
was ultimately claimed by Lord Moreton, for
Gloucestershire, at 460gs.   Fuschia 13th went with
her relative at about half her cost price, to Mr.

W. Ashburner, she was a daughter of the 900 guinea
Fuschia 9th. Cherry Queen, a 1,200 guinea purchase
at Underley, fell on that day in the public's estimation
to a sum of 680gs., but her much admired daughter
was secured by Mr. Drewary for the Duke of Devonshire, at 905gs., then came the tug of war between
Westmorland and Australia for Gazelle 29th, at
last the victory was given in favour of Lord Bective,
but not without a compromise of 455gs., it was then
that I heard a nobleman exclaim, he had bought a
calf of that family for simply nothing, as it was but
little over 100gs. Marchioness of Worcester, a
daughter of Lady Worcester 6th, next made her
appearance in the ring, when a fight for this model
of a shorthorn went by tens and twenties until she
reached 850gs., for the Duke of Devonshire,
Winsonedale 2nd accompanied her to Holker at
550gs., surely it was enough for her as she was but
a plain cow, Fuschia's Duchess immediately entered
the ring as soon as the last lot had departed from it,
Mr. McCullock was not to be denied this gem of
a shorthorn, so she went to Australia with Fuschia
Duchess 2nd, not a despisable companion to travel
with across the wide ocean, they were exactly the same
price, 400gs. each. Mr. Allsopp chimes in for
Kirklevington Princess 4th and takes her to Hindlip,
at 600gs., accompanied by Countess of Worcester,
at 580gs., certainly they are not bad prices to obtain
on the decline of shorthorns, Lord Fitzhardinge and

Lord Feversham each took a daughter of the old matron lot 1., at 400gs. each.   Lord Moreton is not to be disappointed of Siddington 15th at 500gs , Lord Bective has to pay smartly for her last heifer at barely a year old, before taking her to Underly, as the sand did not all run from the glass until Mr. Strafford asked for the name of the buyer at 520gs. The Belle of Worcester was a strange price at eleven months of age, to go to Hindlip at 600gs., yet Mr. Drewry looked with longing eyes, to take her to Holker with her dam.   Lady Gazelle, a four months calf, had to travel to Australia, at a price of 150gs., but all things must have an end so the last female entered into the ring, little more than a suckling youngster and by name Gem of Worcester, a daughter of the Countess', Sir Curtis Lampson promised, Mr. Strafford that he would take her home at 185gs., as everything has an end, so it has a beginning, so the first male animal, 3rd Duke of Hillhurst by name, made his appearance, and gradually advanced in price until the auctioneer declared the last sand had departed from his glass and that Sir Curtis claimed him at 1,550gs., not a low price for a bull in the decline of life, as he was in his 7th year and we may surely add to it by saying it was not a bad average for fifty-two head, when the sum total of £16,194 allowed a division to be made, for each animal, of £311, which sum did not speak much in the favour of fashionable shorthorns going out of repute.

The following day found the company assembled with Mr. Tracey at Eden Bridge, to witness the dispersion of a portion of his herd by Mr. Thornton. Mr. Tracey is evidently a man who takes great interest in the breeding of shorthorns, at the same time he has a style of his own and only a few will admit that he is right in that style of breeding, while his animals contain much good blood and individually not to be despised, yet, they are not such shorthorns as Mr. Fashion would claim as either being purchased or bred by his direction, on the other hand, the writer can speak a word in favour of Mr. Tracey's judgement, as it would be no better than a leap in the dark to depart from his own course of breeding, by purchasing a male for fashion's sake from such animals as I have described in the early part of this chapter, but he has wisely taken a cross from one of the sires to his own cows, the produce being a bull, it is used extensively in his own herd, and he is more sure to get good animals by this mode of breeding as well as being certain to be profitable for the outlay, as I explained in a previous chapter there are different degrees of fashion and it is Mr. Tracey's degree to breed good animals from blood descended from breeders of fashion in their own day, although it may be half a century back, they contained sufficient good breeding to realize an average of £48 6s. 8d.

The 17th of May again finds a fashionable
company gathered together at Buxted, in Sussex, a
place almost roadless, as I remember well, having
some difficulty in getting there from Tunbridge
Wells, but it is an old saying "where there's a will
there's a way," but I think I might safely add
another saying to it, " where there's a fashionable
shorthorn, there will be found a way to it, if this is
not the case visitors would have been scarce both at
Mr. Larking's and Mr. Samuda's, where Mr. Strafford
mounted the rostrum to dispose of fashionable
pedigrees at the latter gentleman's farm, I can
scarcely say fashionable animals, at least what
ought to be fashionable, as an old plain cow made
305gs. and her heifer calf eight months old 410gs.,
a Cherry Duchess made the same sum, but I am
sorry to say that either the Duke or the Duchess
had taken away all the Cherry and left little for the
purchaser beyond the stone, yet Mr. Fashion sold
her daughter for 810gs., but I am afraid he never
had the opportunity of selling many of her produce,
there were many other animals that Fashion bid at
random for; it was then that I pocketed 100gs. profit
in a single heifer, that I had previously purchased,
it was there that I learned a lesson of experience,
not to continue to add Duke upon Duke, but to use
sires from various tribes, still related to each other,
yet at a more distant date.   The average of this
entire herd of forty-three head was £136 7s. 6d.

We pass on until the 21st., when Mr. Thornton and his friends had an invitation to Surrey, where Lady Pigot invited them to luncheon at West Hall, after that was over, Mr. Thornton in his amusing manner of speech, kindly asks them to spend a couple of hours with him in the Park and assist him to value the pictures they would have before them, as well as discuss the merits of Warlaby and Killerby, as it was entirely due to their honour that Victoria Benedictee made 505gs. to Mr. Ackers, the result of the afternoon's pleasure being £63 each for thirty-one animals.

Mr. Thornton is next invited by Mr. Sartoris, of Rushden Hall, in Northamptonshire, to sell his herd, which consisted of fifty-four head, principally of Knightley, Waterloo, Gwynne, and Surmise families, where the last named found a good market by selling for 200gs., 200gs., and 160gs., respectively, to the Duke of Manchester, Sir Curtis Lampson and Sir George Phillips, the Gwynnes too were much appreciated in Northampton, as Mr. Foster and Mr. Loder paid 280gs. each for two sisters, while Lord Bective gave 185gs. for their dam, and Mr. Howard 180gs. for her twin sister, which appeared an exceedingly high price, especially when shorthorns, according to the idea of some, were going out of fashion. The Waterloos also found favour with the public on the 31st of May, as Mr. Lloyd had to pay 465gs. for

Duchess of Waterloo 2nd, before he was allowed to remove her into Surrey, and the Hon. Cecil Duncombe did not find it an easy matter to get hold of her dam for Yorkshire, until she cost him 195gs. without her bull calf, which Col. Levett was glad to secure at 44gs. Fawsley and Milcote each had their admirers and made satisfactory prices, the general result being £91 each, which is not a despisable sum for the decline in shorthorns.

Mr. Green and Mr. Clear had a draught sale at East Donyland in Essex, on the 4th of June, by Mr. Thornton, although the cattle had been crossed with fashionably bred bulls, they were not descended from anything taking enough to bring the average up to £40 each.

Mr. Strafford officiated on the 2nd of July, for Mr. Blundell in Bedfordshire, his animals were principally descended from Sir Charles Knightley's, Mr. Beasley's J.'s, Mr. Bates' Surmises, and Mr. Howard's branch of the Gwynnes. Frisky Gwynne being ten years of age, might be said to sell fairly well at 50gs., while her daughter Fraulein Gwynne realized 100gs. The Surmises, mother and daughter, made 150gs. and 165gs. respectively. The rest of the females did not sell high, but Duke of Oxford 32nd, after being in service two years, reached 235gs., to Mr. Cope in Ireland, the day ended by an average of £48.

Mr. Strafford next travels into Leicestershire to meet his friends at Mr. Holford's on the 4th of the same month, where there was choice material to work upon in the best of Winsomes and Waterloos, as well as the purest of Charmers and American Princesses. They all realized fabulous prices, but the mixed pedigrees were not in request, neither did the visitors care half enough for the fifteen Blanches known by the name of " Brunettes," the property of Sir Curtis Lampson; as good as they were in appearance and their breeding, Mr. Fashion would not touch them, as much as Mr. Strafford used his persuasive powers, it was of no avail, it ended that Sir Curtis had to content himself with £35 10s. for each animal. While Mr. Holford's thirty-seven head made the magnificent sum of £198 11s. each; but look at the difference between Mr. Holford's first animal that entered the ring, and Sir Curtis', the latter brought the low sum of 50gs. for a really grand specimen of a shorthorn; while " Winsome 12th " did not leave until Mr. Strafford announced that she had become Mr. Lloyd's property at 810gs., and her two daughters fell to the bid of Mr. Allsop at 560gs., and 600gs. the younger only six months' old; he also took her companion, " Water Lily 2nd," still younger, at 380gs., a strong price, but she was certainly pretty, as well as being the choice of her family in breeding. Mr. McCullock did not allow Mr. Allsop to have all his own way,

s

so he took the dam with him to Australia at
455gs. Three Princesses also travelled to Hindlip at
nearly 400gs. each, where to-day they are scarcely
worth one-fourth of the money.   A couple of
Charmers were within a hair's breadth of making
200gs. each to Mr. Sheldon. "Viscount Oxford" Mr.
Mackintosh secured at 800gs., which brought the sale
to a successful close.

The following day Mr. Thornton tried his hand
at Elmhurst Hall, near Lichfield, to dispose of
thirty-four animals, the property of Mr. Fox, and
seventeen Blanches belonging to Mr. Hamer, who
received in exchange for them £46 a piece, while Mr.
Fox obtained £104; why is there so great a
difference? simply fashion; where Mr. Hamer bred to
please himself, Mr. Fox tried to please the public by
fashion.   The Red Roses were then in great force at
Elmhurst, Mr. McCulloch was in their favour, and
took them out to Australia at about 300gs. each.
A pretty Waterloo at 225gs., joined them on their
voyage; Kirklevington 25th, although not handsome,
went to Mr. Riggs, in Kent, at 305gs.

England and Ireland were both rushing their
shorthorns into the market, as we find Mr. Thornton
over at our Sister Isle, on August 21st and 23rd,
disposing of selections from Mr. Downing's and
Mr. Chaloner's herds, which were both of Booth
descent, or crossed with Booth bulls, but with

different results, as Mr. Chaloner's barely made 40gs. each, while Mr. Downing's realized over double the amount. Why was this so? Mr. Fashion had again a hand in the matter, which is a clear proof that animals must be in Fashion's favour, or they will not be admitted into Fashion's market.

A few days later Mr. Thornton is in Aberdeenshire, selling the entire herd of one hundred and fifteen animals, the property of the late Mr. Gordon, of Cluny Castle; they were principally of mixed pedigrees, with the exception of a few, and they are not bad to select by the prices they made, as a Booth Waterloo sold for 130gs., and a heifer of the Bliss family for the same price; an average of £30 is the result of Mr. Thornton's journey into Scotland. From there he travels to the Isle-of-Man, to dispose of the Booth bred cattle, the property of Mr. Barnyeat; the herd numbers over eighty, and makes pretty near 40gs. each, which is as much as could be expected in a place so far from any other breeders, yet Mr. Barnyeat had used great care and judgment without too strict economy, in gathering his extensive herd together.

As early as the 4th of September, Mr. Thornton had found his way up into Northumberland, to sell the entire herd of Mr. Wilson, at Shotley Hall; the principal features of the sale were the Wildeyes,

Waterloos and Blanches, Beverleys and Cowslips, the two last tribes having been in Mr. Wilson's possession for many years. The Beverleys having a Bates foundation, he naturally crossed the two families with Bates bulls; the other three are what is termed Bates tribes. The Blanches had a representative in " O. B's Justica," which Mr. MacCulloch secured for Australia at 150gs.; while her daughter, by Royal Killerby, did not reach 50gs., which was evident proof Booth upon Bates was not in request. The Waterloos seemed to have a good demand, but the Wildeyes scarcely knew any bounds to their prices, as the ten females averaged over £400 each; and the good qualities of Duke of Oxford 31st, at four years of age, induced Mr. MacCulloch to pay 435gs. The day wound up with an average of £123 for fifty-six animals; it could not be thought by this result that shorthorns were yet forsaken, not even in that cold northern county.

On the 6th day of September, Mr. Strafford had again the honour of disposing of a selection from a nobleman's herd, who has been, and is still, as staunch an admirer of Bates blood as the auctioneer himself, although that nobleman's residence is situated beneath the dreary hills in Yorkshire, where the herd is kept, it was not thought too far by his fellow noblemen and friends, not only to pay him a visit, but support him in assisting Mr.

Strafford to distribute his animals over the country. Who is the owner of this herd? No less a personage than the Earl of Feversham, whose name has always stood as one of the most prominent in the Kirklevington ranks. The Right Hon. the Earl of Lonsdale claims the highest priced heifer, known by the name of Wild Winsome 3rd, a daughter of Duke of Underley, and Winsome 11th, bred by the Duke of Devonshire, her price is 455gs., before she reached her second birthday. Col. Gunter admired "Winsome Winnie so much, that the auctioneer declared he should take her home, as she was but a tiny calf, and he thought that the Colonel's offer of 200gs ought to suffice. It is evident Lord Morton is not only fond of Kirklevington blood by nature, but name, as he selected "Fair Kirklevington," at three months old, for the Tortworth herd at 275gs. Twentieth Duke of Oxford 28,432, purchased at Holker four years previous for 1,000gs., is now selected by the Rev. H. Beever, at 105gs. to renew his Daisies with Bates blood. Mr. Strafford has the honour, at the conclusion of the day's proceedings, of informing his lordship that a cheque for the value of 80gs. was due for each of the forty-two animals sold.

The County of Devonshire has its representatives in shorthorn breeding, known by the names of Messrs. Scratton, Bassett, Baillie and Pollard,

who each hand over to Mr. Thornton a small
selection from their herds on the 10th day of
September, to be distributed to the best of his
ability, and it too frequently requires more than
ordinary ability to dispose of selections to the
satisfaction of the owners, sometimes for one
reason, and at other times for another; but too
often the animals do not appear to the buyer in as
favourable a light as to the seller; and why is this?
Generally for want of practical knowledge, or in
other words, for want of experience, the weak
points in the animals are not discovered by the
seller until figures do it for them, by letting
out the truth that there is a deficiency to be
seen either in the pedigree, or the animal, by
the practical eye; on the other hand, there are
bargains to be picked up from these selections by
breeders of experience ; the animals are not all sold,
because they are indifferent either in pedigree or
appearance; but that the breeder has too small a
quantity to dispose off to draw a company together,
but if it can be drawn together at all, it will be
accomplished by the ability and influence of Mr.
Thornton, for this reason, the Devonshire breeders
invited him to attend at Newton Abbot and turn
seventy-four head into cash, which he obliged them
by doing in handing over a cheque to the amount of
£1,856 in exchange for their cattle.

Only two days elapsed until he has again the privilege of using his ability and persuasive powers at Messrs. Horswell's, in the same county, by disposing of sixty-four head at an average of £29 each, not a bad price for animals sold in an unprepared state, without any pretensions to fashion beyond Baron Oxford 2nd (23,376), a 500gs. purchase at Mr. Mackintosh's, and now in his thirteenth year, it can not be said that he was thrown away at 81gs.

On September 18th there was a change in prices to what the selections realized that were offered in Devonshire. The day is a glorious one for Mr. Strafford; he appeared younger, and more energetic than he had done for years; he did not forget to remind the visitors that the animals he was then selling were the property of the Duke of Devonshire, and that they were all descendants of cattle belonging to old Tommy Bates; he exclaimed, buy to-day, as the time will come, that they can not be had either for love or money. The day was bright and cheering, not only to the visitors, but to the noble Duke, who had the honour of being owner of one of the best herds in England, and the same honour remains with him still. This was the sale not only of the year, but the best and highest prices (save one) that were ever obtained since shorthorn breeding existed, and that one was the great sale in Scotland, in the year 1875, the property of the

spirited Lord Dunmore, when his average superseded
the Duke of Devonshire by £8, as his selection of
thirty-nine head averaged £672, while the Duke's
for thirty head amounted to £664 each. Here
we had sales of fashionable shorthorns from
herds that had been bred for a number of years,
by perseverance and prudence through experience,
until they had attained a name that echoed from one
end of the nation to the other.

On the following day Mr. Thornton sold the small
but select herd of Mr. Alexander Brogden, M.P.,
which consisted of only fifteen animals, from which
there were three Oxfords, five Princesses, one Waterloo, four Knightleys, and two doubtful breeders. An
Oxford heifer calf realized 955gs. to Mr. Lloyd, and
a yearling Princess 780gs. to Lord Bective, which
brought the average up to £290 each.

After the dispersion of Mr. Brogden's herd, Mr.
Thornton disposed of a selection from Mr. Martin's,
of Bardsea, as well as the entire herd of Mr.
Kennedy, of Ulverston. The animals, the property
of the latter gentleman, were principally descended
from the famous Cassandra, by Miracle, and
Blanche by Belvedere; the Cassandras had scarcely
two crosses alike to follow each other in their breeding, consequently the animals had no distinct
character, and naturally sold for a little money.
The Blanches were just beginning to regain their

Bates character by returning to breed to Bates sires. Col. Gunter purchased the best of the heifers at about 45gs. each. Mr. Kennedy's average barely amounted to £30, while Mr. Martin's reached £57, through judicious management and experience in using appropriate sires to the different branches of females. On the same day, after the completion of the other sales, two Kirklevingtons, a Duchess Nancy, a Duke bull, and an Oxford were next brought into the ring, being imported from Kansas, U.S.A., by Mr. Beatie, and the property of Mr. Crane and Messrs. Avery and Murphy. The choice females and 27th Duke of Airdrie were all purchased by Mr. Lloyd in Surrey. "Fordham Duke of Oxford 4th," by Mr. Botterill, of Wauldby; although they averaged a trifle over £300 each, it appeared to the writer that the shorthorn days were growing darker in the United States by sending their animals to England to turn into cash.

Mr. Strafford is next engaged by Mr. Ladds, of Ellington, to dispose of fifty-six head, which were not bred according to the old man's taste, but contained fragments of breeding in almost every direction, which ended with the price of £32 for each animal.

The following day being the 25th of September, we find that Mr. Thornton congratulated Mr. Polgell on his successful sale of thirty animals in

T

realizing over £60 each, evidently they were good
cattle as the prices testified something beyond their
pedigree.

Another month had at last commenced, and
the sale season not yet over.   Mr. Thornton is
employed, on the third day at Gainsborough,
in Lincolnshire, in disposing of the herd of the late
Mr. Hutton; it is entirely of mixed blood, and the
result is £33 each for fifty animals.   Mr. Lythall
distinguished himself by selling sixty head, the
property of Messrs. Canning and Greenway, at
Snitterfield; the pedigrees were principally of a
local character, and ended in £31 a piece being
made for the whole lot.   On the 17th of October
we again find that Mr. Thornton is engaged, but
this time, at Major Conway's, in North Wales,
where he disposed of his large herd at creditable
prices, which shows the good effect of using good
sires upon ordinary pedigrees without launching
deeply into fashion, as £34 a piece for seventy-five
head cannot help but pay well for breeding.

I have now passed slightly over the principal
sales that took place during the year 1878, when
fashion still held its own, but animals of mixed
blood had a decided falling off.   As I stated in my
introductory chapter, I had no hopes of my pen
being an instrument of information to the practical
breeders, but to the young and inexperienced it

might be the means of preventing them falling into the idea of becoming a practical shorthorn breeder without experience. On the other hand I can well imagine some old breeders on reading these pages muttering to themselves, why has the author troubled himself in relating to us things that we have long known? What is the use of describing the sales that we bought our animals from, we can remember sufficiently well by the experience gained through purchasing entirely by the advice of Fashion. I shall, therefore, now close my chapter, and wander back to the days before Fashion was the principal ruling member in shorthorn society, but Prejudice was even then stiff with old age.

CHAPTER IX.

GAINING EXPERIENCE THROUGH OTHER BREEDERS, FASHION BY INBREEDING INJURIOUS TO THE CONSTITUTION OF ANY ANIMAL, THE FATAL RESULT OF ADDING DUCHESS BLOOD TO VARIOUS TRIBES FOR THE SAKE OF FASHION ALONE.

Having now returned with the explanation of my experience to the year of 1870, when I remember taking a walk upon a hard frosty morning to have a peep at a herd of shorthorns a few days previous to their dispersion by Mr. Strafford. Fancying a heifer calf, I thought she probably might be purchased for about 30gs., but to my astonishment on the day of sale the last sand did not escape from the glass until she had reached 300gs. This was so much to be added to the credit of my experience, after being a shorthorn breeder for ten years on a small scale, and for what I then understood about pedigree cattle, the smaller the better. But only half-a-dozen years more had elapsed before I purchased the same animal that I had previously valued at 30gs. for the sum of 900gs. by private treaty. Is this not a lesson worth reporting upon my early wisdom in shorthorn breeding? It reminds me very forcibly of the son of an old breeder, when

he came into possession of his father's herd, saying
that he would be careful not to make a mistake by
jumbling his pedigrees together as his father had
done, but breed what was most fashionable, and to
be sure he was right, he would first use a sire of
Bates, then one of Booth, upon the same pedigree,
so that it would not matter to him whither of the
twain took the lead, as he would be in possession of
the blood of both. I need hardly relate in this
chapter that animals of his breeding were seldom
inquired after. In the same year as I valued the
300gs. calf so minutely, a nobleman had a sale of
his first selection from his herd, he was not then
young in years, and not far advanced in years of
experience in shorthorn breeding, as he had to be
content with an average of £30 a piece. What do
we find this nobleman doing in the same year, but
improving his herd by purchases? What does he
purchase? Two animals of a Bates tribe, not with
pure Bates crosses, added ever since they left Mr.
Bates, but one bull of Sir Charles Knightley's
breeding, and one of Mason's, or Earl Spencer's
blood, were the last additions made to the dam's
pedigree; but the daughter was by a bull containing a considerable dash of Bates blood, and since
the year 1870 many magnificent animals have been
descended from them by Bates bulls. The writer
had the honour not only of offering over 500gs. for
a daughter from the old cow as well as receiving a

cheerful reprimand for not purchasing her, even at
a higher figure; but what is the value of experience
unless it is made a proper use of ? After the
purchase of these two animals, this nobleman bred
from them for a period of fifteen years, by the most
fashionable bulls, both in breeding and appearance,
but has again resorted to a little admixture in his
latest sire, which has a considerable amount of the
same blood as the original females contained when
he purchased them. This is considered by the
writer worthy of being classed as shorthorn breeding, not simply pedigree making to read well in a
catalogue, but rather, to make the animals attractive
without deteriorating the pedigree in value in the
eyes of a practical breeder.

As the summer advanced, and the days were
becoming warmer with the rays of the sun,
two profitable and interesting sales were held,
principally from two favourite tribes, the Gwynnes
and Charmers, the former the property of Mr.
Howard, of Biddenham, a genuine shorthorn breeder,
not merely a pedigree admirer; the latter gentleman, known by the name of Mr. Tracey, had
evidently a will of his own, or he would not have
had the courage to have used "The Baron (13,833)"
so extensively as he did owing to being a son of Mr.
Booth's Baron Warlaby, from a daughter of Syphls,
by Sir Walter; here we have male and female,

blended together of one tribe, still differently bred
in the latest four generations, followed by Count
Leinster (23,638), a son of Mr. Barnes's Duke of
Leinster, a Mantalini, and the dam of "The Count,"
being Sweetheart 6th, by Mameduke; undoubtedly
the inbreeding, with the suitable infusion of other
pure blood, was the secret of Mr. Tracey's successful
sale in obtaining an average of £86 for forty-four
animals.

Mr. Howard used freely the 5th Grand Duke
upon his Gwynne's, followed by Grand Duke of
Lightburne (26,290), both bulls of fashionable Bates
tribes, yet far from being what the prejudiced
would call pure, but what a practical breeder would
deem prudent to use upon any highly-bred animals
classed as Bates blood. The Duke was by Grand
Duke the 3rd, full of Booth element from Grand
Duchess 9th, by " Prince Imperial," an admirable
Booth and Bates admixture. The younger male in
the herd was from a magnificent daughter of Grand
Duke the 4th, by Grand Duke the 16th, grand-dam
Red Rose, by Marmaduke, by Englishman, by
Paritan, followed by Cambridge Rose the 6th.
Here we have a most successful sale of fifty-three
animals of the Gwynne, Spencer and Knightley
blood, principally by the two sires mentioned, as
Mr. Howard had the pleasure of receiving £71 for
each animal sold; such prices obtained could not be

murmured at, neither can there be much fault found with the breeding of the sires used by Mr. Howard, although containing blood of so many different breeders in their pedigree; yet it is a composition that will bear examining by the critic, and when such names as Bolden, Tanquary and Webb are included in the additions made, his lips are sealed.

The name of Nunwick Hall, near Penrith, will not easily be forgotten by visitors there on the 23rd of September, 1870, who witnessed the dispersion of that magnificent collection of cattle, by Mr. Thornton, the property of Mr. Saunders. Mr. Saunders's father was a great admirer of good animals well descended, but without being prejudiced to any special pedigree. He selected, in the formation of his herd, the blood of Sir Charles Knightley and Mr. Crofton, and we also find that the memory of Mr. Bates was not forgotten, by the purchases of several Waterloos, as well as Wildeyes 19th, by Lablache (16,453), the dam of " Wildeyes Duchess," by 9th Grand Duke, which was thought not only good enough to purchase for Canada at 275gs., but to re-purchase by Lord Dunmore and travel back into Scotland, where she was sold in the 1875 sale for 480gs., to Mr. Wilson, of Shotley Hall, at ten years of age; her three daughters, all by Duke bulls, Wildeyes Bright, Sparkling Eyes, and Blythsome Eyes, realized the handsome figure of

1,405gs.; they were sold equally as much by their
merits as their pedigree; they had but two Duke
crosses added since Mr. Bolden's Lablache and the
Troutbeck Strawberry bull, Solon (13,766). Is
this not a sufficient proof that it is not necessary to
breed too closely, to realise paying prices for good
animals, well descended, without being strictly line
bred? Take, for instance, Waterloo 36th, by Earl
of Eglington (23,832), selling for 475gs., to Lord
Bective, while her yearling sister made 300gs., to
Mr. Cochrane; and Waterloo 40th, an exceedingly
handsome heifer, for the same sum at twelve
months old, to the Rev. P. Graham; she was not
only white, but by Edgar (19,680), a bull with a
pedigree that was not worshipped by the purist; can
the writer not say something in favour of Edgar? He
was, as an animal, the best we had then in England,
an easy winner at the Royal, and descended from
Mr. Crofton's Elvira, with an addition of Bates,
Booth and Knightley. Earl of Eglington was a son
of 10th Grand Duke, the best of the Grand Dukes
I ever remember seeing; his dam, Lady Elvira, a
daughter of Lord Oxford (20,214), thought by many
good judges the best Oxford bull ever seen at
Holker; grand-dam, Countess Emma, which was
also the grand-dam of the famed Edgar. How
could such an alliance fail to produce good animals, by
the service of Earl of Eglington, upon Edgar's
daughters? Altho' Waterloo 37th, which made

v

500gs., was by Royal Cambridge (25,009), he, like
the preceding sires named, had an abundance of
personal merit, beyond the aristocratic lineage of
his parents; and what were they but Grand Duke
the 4th, sire of the 10th, and the elegant Moss
Rose, which realized 350gs., in her thirteenth year;
she was a daughter of that magnificent bull, Marmaduke (14,897), a son of the 650gs. Duke of
Gloucester, from a Gwynne cow, but even if he was
only a descendant of one of Mr. Troutbeck's hardy
constitutioned animals, Col. Penant thought him
equal to 400gs., when he purchased him to mate
with his Cherries and Oxfords, the grand-dam of
Royal Cambridge, being Cambridge Rose the 6th,
bred by Mr. Bates. The pedigree of Waterloo 37th
reads without showing any direct change of blood
in any of the generations; but without going into
its breeding minutely, there is Cleveland Lad, no
less than three times, Prince Imperial twice, and
Grand Duke the 3rd twice, leaving to one side the
mixed blood of the dam of Marmaduke. Waterloo
37th, bred in the hands of Captain Oliver, Grand
Duke of Waterloo, the sire of Grand Duke the 31st,
which realized 1,550gs., at Sholebroke, to Lord
Bective, who purchased him with a view of the
compound mixture contained in the Waterloo
pedigree having an influential effect upon his inbred tribes. The result of Mr. Saunders' breeding
ended with the proceeds of the day by his thirteen

Waterloos making nearly £200 each, three Wildeyes £153, sixteen Knightleys £70, fourteen Emmas, or Crofter's blood, £66, and six Gwynnes £55, or a general average of £96 for sixty-one animals, speaks volumes in favour of Mr. Saunders' judgment as an experienced breeder free from prejudice.

The herds that I have alluded to, in their style of breeding, in this chapter, were all brought to a successful issue by the owners striking out a course of their own, and pursuing it, they were neither led entirely by fashion or prejudice, but preferred their own judgment in preference to the latter, which enabled them to admit sufficient of the former, to make their breeding both pleasant and profitable. Messrs. Saunders and Tracey each bred their own sires, by sending their choicest females on a visit to other herds; while Mr. Howard pursued another course, by purchasing males of individual merit, of good blood, but throwing aside the prejudice of having them strictly line bred, yet the greatest possible care was taken in their selection.

As the summer advances after the spring, and autumn is sure to follow after the summer, at such a time Mr. Thornton officiated, upon one of these dark autumn days, at Badmington, in disposing of the entire herd of Mr. Butler; but the principal feature in the sale was the ambition to secure a Darlington cow, or heifer, but there were many visitors on the same errand from different parts of the world, as Mr. Pearce, from California, was a strong rival against the home county, it was evident he would have his way, in taking a couple across the Atlantic, which cost him considerably over 100gs. each; Mr. Davis taking the old Matron when fourteen years old at 65gs., and two of her daughters at more than double the money, but shortly after sold them to Mr. Thompson, who now holds a round number of the family, in addition to his Barringtons, as a select little herd, and crossing them with Bates bulls, yet, not forgetting to bear in mind that a good animal looks quite as well in his pasture as a strictly pure pedigree appears upon paper. The writer remembers well, giving the auctioneer a commission of 35gs. for Darlington 19th, as she had got an extra Bates cross added more than her relations, since the old veteran gave his advice to buy "Pretty Maid," the ancestor of the Darlington tribe; but it was evident there were others besides myself that felt covetous to possess the calf, as she did not leave the ring until she was claimed by Mr. Davis at 85gs.

It was as far back as the days that I am speaking of in the present chapter, when breeders of a certain class began to calculate upon the value of a shorthorn according to the number of either Booth or Bates crosses they had in succession in the latest generations, it was considered by them as safe an investment as placing their money in the Bank of England, to pay 20gs. for each additional pure cross added to a pedigree, providing that purity was either of Bates or Booth blood; should any other blood be added, after a number of crosses of either of the two former, it was looked upon as losing both principal and interest. What reply does Experience give on the result of such a course of breeding? I will take the Cherry Duchesses as the first experiment. Cherry, by Pirate, was known to be an exceedingly grand cow in her day, as well as many of her descendants in the late Col. Cradock's hands. Brandy Cherry, by Sheldon (8,537), was selected by Mr. Bolden as a good sort to cross with Bates blood; the first calf, by Grand Duke, was named Cherry Duchess, the 2nd, own sister to the first, was considered much better, and from her descends the once popular Cherry Duchess family, Cherry Duchess 2nd, was put by Mr. Bolden to 2nd Grand Duke, the produce being Cherry Duchess 3rd; in due time this young heifer was put to 3rd Grand Duke, which resulted in the birth of the fine cow, Cherry Duchess 6th. Mr. Bolden tries the experiment of a double cross with 3rd Grand Duke, which proves to be Cherry Duchess 8th, by no means as good as her dam; fortunately, before the close of her life, she falls into hands that had a suitable bull named General Napier, by Grand Duke the

4th, from a Princess cow; the reunion of the
Duchess and Princess blood restored the good
qualities (lost by too much repetition of the Bank of
England securities) in the birth of a lovely heifer
named Cherry Princess; Lord Dunmore takes her
into Scotland at 500gs. when a yearling, and returns
her to Lord Bective, in calf to Baron Oxford 5th, at
810gs., which resulted in the birth of Cherry Queen,
one of the handsomest animals ever bred of the
family. Does not realizing 1,200gs. in the Underley
sale speak sufficient for her good qualities? I will
next point out the different result from her senior
sister, with a 5th Grand Duke cross. Being on a
visit in the Midland Counties, I passed an interesting hour inspecting a fashionably bred herd of
shorthorns, a heifer in the yard taking my fancy
beyond where the aristocratic young lady was
standing, I speedily moved her out of the way and
exclaimed, if she was not an Irish she was good
enough to be one; not many months later her
pedigree was sold for 410gs; of course, her new
owner must put her to a Duke bull to make her a
safe investment, as the produce would then be
exceedingly valuable; fancy, six Duke crosses upon
the inbred Cherry pedigree; the calf proved to be a
heifer, but I will not commit myself by saying she
was as good as her dam, but at any rate, with the
idea of breeding a good one at the last, she was also
mated with a Duke of no mean repute; the calf,

again a heifer, with seven Duke crosses in succession, surely must be hard to surpass in merit. For some reason, that I am not able to explain, the breeder sold her, shortly after this highly descended animal was disposed of by Mr. Thornton, when her late owner was quietly looking on as the last sand departed from the glass at the price of 41gs., apparently not showing the least signs of regret that he had seen the last result by the union of the seven Dukes; although he had lost sight of them, he had found a lesson by experience, that even seven could not restore the constitution that one had shattered. When a building of any kind is fast mouldering to decay, is it not much wiser to rebuild from the foundation than attempt to repair the decayed material? May I ask my readers if it would be far out of place to adopt the same course in restoring the weakened constitution? Has not the disease been creeping stealthily along for years past, either by prejudice or fashion, into many that are called fashionable tribes? Will not the day soon arrive that it will be too late for repairing, and the constitution destroyed from the foundation? Some might say that Grand Duke 3rd had sufficient change of blood in his sire, 2nd Duke of Bolton, it is quite true that it would be so, in an ordinary case; but suppose a physician mixes his medicine in every way suitable for the disease he is treating, but should he give his patient a double dose, it

might have a poisonous effect. It is the writer's
opinion that the double cross of 3rd Grand Duke
was injurious to the Cherry Duchesses, although he
was by 2nd Duke of Bolton, a son of Grand
Duke; the dam of 3rd Grand Duke was also by
Grand Duke, from Duchess 51st, by Cleveland Lad,
own brother to the sire of Grand Duke; 2nd Grand
Duke was by 4th Duke of York, a son of 2nd Duke
of Oxford, from the sister to Cleveland Lad; the
dam of 4th Duke of York was Duchess 51st, by
Cleveland Lad, the grand-dam of Grand Duke 3rd.
The inbreeding previous, in each of the Grand
Duke's pedigrees, has been named fully in my
remarks upon early breeders. Allow me to pass on
and make a few observations upon the other
descendants of Cherry Duchess 6th with only one
cross of 3rd Grand Duke, in the hands of the late
Lord Penryhn; the first calf is by Marmaduke, the
400gs. bull, from a Gwynne cow, by Duke of
Gloucester, and named Cherry Duchess 9th, the
dam of the 13th, by 3rd Duke of Wharfdale, which
cost the writer 555gs.; she was truly a grand cow,
with a constitution unpenetrable by either wind or
storm, her daughter, Cherry Duchess 21st, by 11th
Grand Duke, bred in the hands of Mr. Sharpley,
Cherry Arch Duchess, by 27th Grand Duke, she is now
as grand a cow as any breeder would desire to look
upon, the constitution has been saved through
Marmaduke, so that it requires no immediate restora-

tive. There are also descendants from Cherry
Duchess 6th, bred in two other different ways;
firstly, her daughter, the 11th, is by that splendid
bull Duke of Geneva (19,614); two daughters of
the 11th are by 11th Grand Duke and 2nd Duke of
Grafton (25,968), a Duchess Nancy Bull, from the
produce of the latter; the only descendants remain at
Penryhn; Cherry Duchess 9th., own sister to the 6th,
went to Sholebroke, at the same time as the latter went
to Penryhn, and very little was left to her credit at
the winding up of the Sholebroke herd, beyond one
good cow with the mixture of Cherry Butterfly
(23,550), son of Romulus Butterfly (18,741), the
Best of Townley's composition; while there remains
but a single remnant from Cherry Duchess 22nd,
bred in the direct line with Duke crosses, which is
Grand Cherry Duchess of Brailes 3rd, by Duke of
Rothesay (36,534), she has the honour of being the
dam of two daughters, also by Duke bulls, which I
trust may have strength to keep up the family
name of Cherry Duchess.

What family made more rapid strides than the
Florentia's after they left the hands of Mr. Rich.
Duke upon Duke was the directory for a Bates
breeder to make a great name. But what tribe
fell away more quickly than the descendants of the
beautiful Lady Maynard, although bred according
to the direction of fashion? The Gazelles, once so

W

popular, owing to being related through their sires
to the Duchesses, have they not gradually but surely
fallen to pieces? Was their value not fictitious,
simply because they claimed relationship to several
Dukes? Were they valued according to their
personal excellence, or purity of descent? I am
afraid that the Bank of England investment was no
better either in the Florentias or the Gazelles, than
it was with the Cherry Duchesses. Were they not
all esteemed far beyond their value in the com-
mercial market, which is in reality the only place
to find the true value of Fashion? Were there
not several other tribes that suffered either by
Fashion or Prejudice? for instance, the Princesses,
were once thought good enough to improve the constitution of the Duchesses, but at last they were bred
in and in, until there were but half-a-dozen left in
England, and supposed to be valuable, because
their numbers were so reduced by inbreeding. Are
they the kind of animals England requires for her
posterity? The writer might venture to say that
the Gwynnes, from same foundation, yet held
neither by fashion's favour, nor bound by prejudice,
are more what our thickly populated nation admires
as staunch against the bitter easterly winds,
and more liberal suppliers of milk and butter, in
addition to being strong supporters of the demand
required for the roast beef of old England. Is this
not what the present generation boasts of in the

shorthorns? Is it not what our forefathers cultivated them for? Ought it not to be for the same reason that the present and rising generation should cultivate the shorthorn in all its usefulness, and not to destroy it by being bred as a slave to Fashion?

CHAPTER X.

THE DATES OF THE RISE AND FALL IN SHORTHORNS,
COMPARING THEM TO TRAVELLING OVER A
MOUNTAIN, VARIOUS TRIBES OF CATTLE WORTHY
OF SELECTION TO BREED FROM, NOT NECESSARY
TO BREED GOOD CATTLE FOR THE SAKE OF
FASHION, BUT FOR SAME REASON AS THEY WERE
ORIGINALLY INTRODUCED BY EARLY BREEDERS,
A GOOD HERD CAN BE PROFITABLY BRED BY
CAREFUL SELECTION FROM DAIRY COWS, ANIMALS
TO BE KEPT IN A NATURAL STATE TO BE PRO-
DUCTIVE AS BREEDERS AND MILKERS.

The last four chapters that I have written contain a short account of the experience witnessed
during the rise and fall of fashionable shorthorns
in price and popularity. In the present chapter I
shall endeavour to compare the difference in value
during the last eighteen years, by showing how,
and when they rose, and in what years they fell.
In the year 1868, through the scarcity of food, the
prices of shorthorns became exceedingly low, but
the following spring brought a considerable revival,
and when the writer looks back to that date, it
reminds him very forcibly of travelling over an
exceedingly high mountain, which was very

difficult to ascend to the highest point, but when it was once reached was comparatively level for some distance before beginning to descend into the valley, a part of the journey that was apparently accomplished with the greatest ease, but descending so rapidly from such a lofty position, left upon the writer the impression that even ascending with difficulty gave a larger amount of pleasure than the rapid descent.

Can I not compare travelling over that mountain in some degree to shorthorn breeding during the period spoken of, as it certainly has been to many breeders a source of trial, the rapid fall in prices after so many expensive purchases have been made? In the years 1869, 1870, 1871 and 1872, there was a gradual rise in the shorthorn market, especially for such animals as were in Fashion's favour; 1873, 1874, 1875 and 1876, brought them to the highest point ever attained since the days of the Brothers Colling; 1877 and 1878 realized some miraculous prices, but here the buyer and seller halted between two opinions, when all appeared to be stationary, there was no ascending higher, not even by Fashion's favour; in 1879 and 1880 it was evident there was a downward tendency which caused many a heavy heart to the extensive purchaser; many sold out rather than risk holding on to see the end of the downfall, others purchased and said, surely they cannot fall much lower; in 81 and 82 sales were frequently held which brought many new beginners into the market, who said certainly we have secured great bargains, as the prices of our animals are fully one-third less than they were two years ago; we cannot be wrong in purchasing fashionable pedigrees, but men of experience were more weary and soon found that the years 1883 and 1884 would still carry them lower and lower; yet there were new beginners in young noblemen, the squires, and the spirited tenant farmers to purchase the most fashionable tribes, as they imagined they were sure to pay; but some doubt then arose as to which were fashionable; in 1883 and 1884 fashion had changed, and will change again, as many familiar tribes once so fashionable and popular to the public. The years 1885 and 1886 brought them to the bottom of the hill of Temptation, there many of them will be gathered up and restored to their former position as a tribe by breeders of experience, and are there not many besides the writer, who have witnessed the eight years of ascendancy in the value of shorthorns, also the two stationary ones, as well as the eight years of descendancy which have taught many valuable lessons that will be remembered, that shorthorns are not to be bred for the sake of pedigree alone, but for the same purpose as they were a century back by breeders of that date, in trying to gain experience by breeding such animals as deservedly won the name of " The

Improved Shorthorn?" It is true, they at last bred them in and in beyond what was either profitable or good for the improvement of the animal; but are they not lessons of experience recorded for our advantage? Did not the eight years of ascendency in the value of shorthorns teach us many a bitter lesson? The two stationary ones, were they not a warning to the experienced; and the eight years of descendency, have they not taught lessons that few want repeating? Purchases were made during that period that changed the inexperienced to be experienced. Have not too many purchased and bred by Fashion and Prejudice that caused them some difficulty in climbing the mountain of ambition in hopes of reaching its summit by Fashion's favour? They had heard that there was a rich valley beyond, for those that carried out short-horn breeding in its strictest purity, but the writer has seen by experience that the rich portions of the valley are only to be obtained by the breeders of the present fashion, and can only be secured by breed-ing so near a precipice as to be in continual danger of losing constitution and being prolific; then why venture to climb the mountain of ambition in anticipation of reaching so uncertain a point, by inbreeding too closely allied to Prejudice and Fashion? Although the writer has been a success-ful fashionable breeder, it was not attained without years of perseverance, by experience through lessons gained by the humble Buttercup he then possessed, and the despised Princess Helena. Has he not spoken of the rising and falling of the once popular Cherry Duchesses, Gazelles, Florentias and Princesses that were bred entirely by Fashion, and their owners being somewhat prejudiced against any other blood being admitted, which was to a certain extent the cause of their fall. Are there not now various other tribes which are bred so near the precipice as to be in continual danger of falling over, simply by being prejudiced against other breeders for fear of displeasing Fashion? Has not the constitution been weakened? Does it not show the visible signs by its diminutiveness? Surely many other families of shorthorns will be lost sight of in future years if they are not allied with alien blood. Why be so prejudiced after seeing the fatal effect of too close breeding by the experience of others?

Are not there still many good animals descended from Hartforth Cherries, which have not been bred in danger of the precipice to fall over and receive internal injuries? Are not there yet many meritorious animals descended from " Princess," by Favourite. which have not been a slave to Fashion? Are not there descendants of the once famed " Lady Maynard " worthy of cultivation? Have we not many representatives of the once popular Gazelles, which took the late Mr. Bowley the best part of his shorthorn career to bring to perfection? Surely there must be some remnant of this once fashionable tribe that is desirable for a new beginner to breed from. Have we not yet some branch of the once esteemed Daisies that are tempting to give a prominent position? Certainly there are still many branches of the various families of the late Sir Charles Knightley's worthy of remembrance. Are not there also several old tribes, once so popular at Studley, Killerby and Warlaby, that can be restored to their former prosperity, even if they do contain a little admixture? Where are the descendants of the late Mr. Maynard's fine cattle that produced such wonderful steers? Are they not worth seeking? Have we no remnants from many other breeders of the past? Yes! far too numerous to particularize in so small a volume. By an experienced hand there are those able to breed such animals that are deserving the name of "The Improved Shorthorn." They may not stand in the first ranks in the sale ring, but are capable of breeding good animals by a prudent selection of sires; it is true, they will require carefully cultivating through having such a compound mixture of blood descended from so many different types; the breeder must fix the character of the animal he wishes to produce by the sires he selects, as it is undoubtedly a fact that like begets like. The next cross is even more

x

difficult than the first; to improve upou an old tribe that contains so many varieties of blood, the second sire must be sure to possess all the good qualities of the first, in addition to au improvement upon his deficieuces; then there is little fear of the result in the second generation being of one uniform character. I have often noticed in ordinary dairy herds bred for generations upon the same farm, that the animals of each age are frequently like sisters; and why is this? because they are all bred in a similar way, and the only difference to pedigreed cattle they are not registered, but are of one blood, and the whole herd related to each other. It was but yesterday I glanced over a class of cattle of this description; in speaking to the owner, and asking him how they were bred, the reply was in his county brogue, "tha's all bred one way; I buys my bulls with pedigree but never a cow, cos' I often notice pedigree men never get rich." I could not but smile, although talking to a comparative stranger, and on turning away, thought his name surely must be Mr. Prejudice, as his wisdom appeared to be wrapped up in himself and his riches. But I must now move northwards with my experiences, and leave the Midlands and its cattle behind me, to speak of one, not only a nobleman by birth, but by nature; even in his youthful days he had an acquired taste for short-horns, but like others of his years that were inexperienced, frequently purchased the best animal, irrespective of pedigree, at each sale, and by such purchases built up a herd only to throw it down again. It has been re-built by the hand of Experience, and is now not only one of the finest herds in England, but in the world. It is not built up entirely by pedigree or Fashion, but by the practical art of shorthorn breeding in producing good animals well descended to meet the present market. I have often conversed and even expressed my opinion freely upon paper to its owner, and the name of that owner is no less a personage than the Right Hon. Earl Bective, of Underley Hall, who has ultimately selected his families from the Grand Duchesses, Princesses, Red Roses, Darlingtons and Underley Darlings descended from Mr. Langston's Turk's Darling by Royal Turk 16875. The Grand Duchesses are bred on the lines of fashion, Bates upon Princess, or Bates and Princess upon Bates. The Red Roses were somewhat bred away from fashion before coming to Underley, but are one of the tribes that may, at a future day, be brought into the first ranks. The Darlingtons are, as a rule, heavy fleshed good animals, and have long been favourites at Underley; but the Underley Darlings, strictly speaking, are a family that his lordship has kept entirely for its usefulness, both in the dairy and as breeding animals without any pretence whatever as to

fashion beyond breeding a male that will realize
100gs. as a yearling; not a bad sort of fashion
as the result of the union with high class
bulls, but it is not necessary for the union
to be always with a Duke, as the male
produce from this family are sold entirely upon
their personal excellences.   Was this not also
why Mr. Charles Colling stored his Duchess
tribe above others? and also why Mr. Bates purchased Young Duchess at his sale?   Was it not
also for the same reason that Mr. Bates used sires
from this tribe in preference to any others?   By
valuing this family beyond its personal merit, did
his herd not deteriorate?   Have not various breeders,
during the eighteen years of the rising and falling
in the value of shorthorns, improved many old
tribes by Duke crosses; yet, by seeing that marked
improvement, did some of them not become a little
prejudiced against any other sires but a Duke intermingling with them?   I have received but the shake
of the head for an answer, when asking an old
breeder if he did not think it high time for a little
change in his herd, after four or five successive
crosses from Duke bulls had been admitted.   It is
true, Fashion rose in value during the eight years of
ascendency, but after their expiration was not there
a halt between two opinions?   When it had
gradually but surely to give way in the eight
years of descendency in a great measure to personal

merit; but the next question that arises is how are we not only to obtain, but keep it in our possession, only by practical experience in breeding highly descended shorthorns that have been for years, and have still, a superiority in their personal appearance? It is not absolutely necessary that they should have passed through the hands of either Booth or Bates, or any other renowned breeder of the past, to be good animals, then why venture to attempt to travel over the mountain of Ambition to reach the valley of extreme Fashion, which can be only obtained by travelling so near a precipice as to be in danger of shattering the constitution and running the risk of losing the dairy and breeding propensities?

Some strict admirers of Fashion may say we have passed through a long period of agricultural depression, and the demand for all productions are at ruinous prices. True, things are, and have been, exceedingly low, but what meets the market better than a good article, especially in a good shorthorn, that can be manufactured at very little more cost than the ordinary dairy cow, even by the smallest capitalist; they are within the reach of any enlightened tenant farmer, but too far away for the prejudiced to see that there is an opportunity before them to improve their cattle, for fear they should have to alter their mode of breeding; but perhaps

what is more important still, their way of thinking
that pedigree men never get rich, and dare not
venture to go out of their ordinary course.   But
there is still another way open for them, that might
help to gather riches rather than scatter, by following the example of the late Mr. Richard Stratton
who persevered in breeding from dairy cows by
pedigree bulls, until they became eligible for the
herd book, and in 1868 sold one hundred head of
this description when cattle were far from being in
high request; yet a bull calf at four months old
reached 30gs., descended from Moss Rose, by
Phœnix 6290, a pair of animals as highly appreciated by the Stratton family as Hubback and Young
Duchess were by Mr. Bates.   A second selection
was again offered for competition in 1871, when
fifty-five animals were disposed of by Mr. Thornton,
all descended from the selected Dairymaid, when
forty-four females averaged £32 19s. 4d., and
eleven bulls £37 19s. 9d.; surely such prices are
tempting to turn the most prejudiced in favour of the
improved registered shorthorn.   In such a course
of breeding as Mr. Stratton pursued, there is no
danger of falling over the precipice and injuring either
constitution or their dairy properties, as the weak
and inferior animals, as well as the bad milk pro-
ducers, would naturally be discarded; three important
points to bear in mind in breeding either fashionable
or animals of lower degree, as the mean looking

beast is liable to a weak constitution, and moderate milkers, as a rule, are slow breeders ; three things not desirable in any case, and to avoid them all it requires the strictest attention being paid in selection of sires from robust well developed animals with all the milking propensities required in a shorthorn, and above all shun the animals that have been fed unnaturally, as natural food and shelter is what they require for both health, milk, and breeding ; they ought not to be kept as hot-house plants for nine months in the year, but allowed to roam over the distant pastures for at least that period, except such as are in milk, and young calves, as a quantity of milk cannot be produced without sufficient warmth, neither is the growth of the suckling to be obtained without it.

Again in purchasing highly descended or fashionably bred animals I have found by experience that the constitution suffers considerably by the removal from a southern to a northern or eastern climate, where the bitterness of the winds is sure to search out their weak points ; on the contrary the removal of animals from a northern to a southern one has usually a beneficial effect. It behoves every breeder to produce such animals as are best adapted for where he resides and the farm he occupies ; but few will take heed and understand until they have learned a costly lesson from the book of Experience. There is nothing so ruinous to the milking properties as high feeding in youth, even from the best of dairy cows and by a sire from a good milker, as I have myself entirely destroyed the milking capacities of several such animals simply by feeding for exhibition, which is sure to be fatal in the second generation of riotous living, if fortunate enough to escape it in the first. Some years ago I had a shorthorn cow that gave her twenty quarts of milk daily after calving a pretty heifer calf, which of course must be exhibited as she was pretty, not pretty enough to be any more than commended, and not pretty enough even for the dairy, as I cannot remember her ever giving more than eight quarts per day, and not any length of time so large a quantity. About the same time I was also in possession of another excellent dairy shorthorn, at least a good cow and fair milker, that gave her sixteen quarts per day after giving birth to a calf, and a reasonable quantity for the following nine months ; she also calved a a pretty heifer, which of course in due time must be exhibited and made fat too ! or it would be useless for that purpose ; she managed also to get a commendation at two or three exhibitions, besides giving her owner considerable trouble in getting her to breed, but at last produced a nice roan heifer, which he contrived to kill at a few days old through giving her milk from another cow, for the only reason that her dam did not even give the colour of

milk, but naturally she gave a few drops of nutrit-·
ious food for the calf, which I did not then understand, for want of experience, that it was the proper
food to sustain life in the new-born animal, but it
taught me a two-fold lesson, firstly in feeding the
heifer two years for exhibition, and only having the
honour of receiving commendation tickets as the
reward; I also remember very correctly that I
imagined she ought to have had something more, but
supposed the Committee had not selected very good
judges that season, as they left both myself and the
heifer out in the cold; secondly, I found by losing
the calf that my early wisdom could not supersede
nature, so in the future I did not try to dictate to
her how to feed a newly-born animal, but contented
myself in pocketing the loss, though gaining a
lesson by the experience. A third shorthorn that I
procured gave me a similar quantity to the last.
She also bred a heifer which I thought rather a good
one and unfortunately a winner for calves, which
was an inducement to go on pampering and feeding
until she herself produced a calf, but not milk;
to save the calf I allowed it to have nature's
food and persevered day by day in drawing at the
dam until she gave nearly two quarts per day.
She bred but three calves and was afterwards hopeless as a breeder; I had previously sold the constitution
and milk of two of the animals to Fashion, I then
sold the last of the three and their produce, as I

Y

began to learn, by paying dearly for lessons, that
bad milkers were slow breeders, which made me
begin to consider if I was acting wisely by ex-
hibiting at Agricultural Shows, after purchasing
highly descended animals at long prices for breeding
purposes, as I had certainly destroyed both the
milking and breeding capabilities of many that I
had exhibited or their produce, and even more, their
health in many instances by over feeding in loose
boxes, or stalls, and afterwards exposing them to the
inclemency of the weather; not recklessly, nor
even in a careless manner, but reducing the artificial
food by degrees until their diet became the ordinary
produce of the farm, one lesson after another
taught me that all breeding animals should be kept
in a natural state, so I determined that for the
future I would leave the losses by injudicious
feeding for exhibitions to parties who could better
afford to receive them.

As there are various points of merit in the
animals and the pedigrees, so there are in the
breeders, but the same point is not always equally
prominent. The names of Warlaby, Dereham
Abbey, Holker, Berkeley, Underley, Kingscote,
Lathom, or Tortworth, are not stamped upon every
herd, but each owner must prepare his own stamp or
type to bring him into a prominent position as a

breeder, and this can only be done step by step as he gains experience.   A prominent position as a purchaser may be obtained for money, but as a breeder—Never !

CHAPTER XI.

DIFFERENT DEGREES IN WRITERS COMPARED TO SHORT-
HORN BREEDERS, GENERAL REMARKS UPON THE
PAST AND PRESENT.

As I am now fast drawing to a close with my
experiences upon shorthorns, it is only natural
to have a desire to oblige as many of my readers
as I possibly can, especially the friendly advisers
mentioned in an earlier chapter; but I am afraid
that I have already displeased the first by
deviating from them in the second part of my
history, and the demand of the last that I should
write a sensible one is of so gigantic a nature that
I dare not promise to grant his request; but that of
two others, one of which desires that it should not
all be upon shorthorns, but intermixed with other
experiences, and his friend, who asked to give it a
jovial 'turn, I will try to oblige in the concluding
chapter; but the fourth and fifth are so contradic-
tory to each other in their advice that I really cannot comply with the wishes of both, as one tells me
to put things seriously before them, and his
opponent says, if you do, the people will never read
them! The remembrance of these remarks teaches
me a lesson of experience, that even a writer has

difficulties to contend with as he passes through life, which makes him pause for a few moments with pen in hand, before proceeding further, and ponder over the beauties of nature as he observed in the rustic oak that has stood for ages, the stately elm that has sprung up more quickly and even superseding it in grandeur, beyond them both stands the graceful lime, adored by every true lover of nature, they are all in equal possession of the much admired tinted leaf which shall so soon fall from the lofty branches and be looked upon as no more than an encumbrance to the ground, which reminds the writer that his experiences may be interesting and instructive to some, but to others will be held in no higher estimation than the fallen leaves. This is the only reward that can be hoped for by an inexperienced writer, then why should the inexperienced breeder anticipate the same success for his labours as the man of experience. Can I not compare a practical writer of fifty years standing to the matured oak which is naturally possessed of great solidity, and a fashionable one of somewhat more recent date to the stately elm, and are there not other authors of still more refined taste, whose works are looked upon to be as perfect as the graceful lime? Do they not teach me to ask the question—What am I in comparison to any of the three as a writer?—Simply a scholar under the guidance of Experience.

But I must return to shorthorn lore,
And speak of Nature's charms no more;
And write upon them only at my leisure,
For fear of provoking shorthorn displeasure.

As there are different degrees in writers, so
there are in shorthorn breeders, but the same
breeder cannot attain perfection in every degree,
but must content himself by being successful in
that line of breeding he has mapped out for
himself. It is not necessary that he should attain
the celebrity of a Collings, Bates, or a Booth
to be a successful breeder, but to move prudently
along by perseverance until he gains the knowledge
through experience, how to build up a herd
judiciously upon the foundation he has selected, no
matter whether that foundation has been in existence for a century, or that it cannot boast of any
descent beyond personal appearance. Have we not
examples before us of breeders of the past, how
they founded our popular tribes. Did not the late
Mr. Richard Booth after his sale at Studley in 1834,
exclaim to a well-known visitor, in speaking of the
famous Isabella, by Pilot (496), "upon that single
thread of a calf the future of my herd depends ";
how was she bred beyond to make her so attractive
to the eye of the veteran breeder? Simply by
Agamemnon (9), grand-dam by a bull of Mr.
Burrell's, of Burdon. When Mr. Thos. Bell could
not find a customer for the ancestors of the Oxfords,

did not Mr. Bates come to the rescue, and declare
that from her he would breed a Royal winner. She
had then but two registered crosses, Matchem, and
Young Wynyard. When we see such things that
were predicted fifty years back carried out so successfully in our day, is not there still room for new
tribes to be founded. When Mr. Bates purchased
the original heifers from which the Kirklevingtons
and the Craggs are descended, they were nothing more
than two ordinary beasts, selected in Northallerton
market for their good looks, from the herd of the
famed Anthony Maynard; but do not their descendants rank as animals of fashion? What were
the Hecubas and the Paulines in the days of the
late Messrs. Richard and John Booth in comparison
to what they are to day? They were then simply
classed as dairy cows, and the Christon were
barely recognized as shorthorns, but are at the
present time one of the most popular families at
Warlaby, surpassing many in merit of the old
established and inbred tribes. The writer paid
several visits there in the days of the late Mr. Thomas
Booth, and had frequent conversations with him
respecting the rising and falling of which were most
popular families at Studley, Killerby and Warlaby,
how they rose by their purity in the eyes of the public,
and how they were sacrificed to in-breeding by
being unfruitful, which left no other course open to
him but to replenish his herd by purchases from

the original families allied with other blood, or to
prepare new tribes for Coates' from the dairy cows.
The former course being adopted in preference to
the latter has to some extent restored Warlaby to
its former fame and numbers.   It is not Warlaby
or Kirklevington alone that has allowed various
tribes to diminish, but every breeder who has sold
himself to be prejudiced against the admittance
of the necessary change required.

Some might argue that families have gone down
in public estimation through the prices realized at
the present day, but this is no criterion to be based
upon, as the writer remembers having a cow that
cost him 500 gs. ; her first calf realized 610 gs.
before three months of age, two years later her
yearling son made 52 gs., and his own sister,
equally as well bred and superior as an animal to
the previous one sold, realized but 170 gs., at a little
over six months; thirdly, her next yearling heifer
made but 54 gs., and her bull calf 20 gs. ; the old dam
herself went at 53 gs., on the same day.   It is an
old story that what an article brings by auction is
its value, but this argument will not hold good in all
cases, as the 610 gs. calf was not worth half the
sum obtained, the 170 gs. and the 54 gs. heifers
were really worth more, and have since made
grand cows and continued to breed good animals,
while their sister was purchased by a fit of excite-

ment alone, leaving her value as to breed and
personal appearance in the background, she has
departed without leaving any issue in return. Such
purchases were often made not only by myself but by
others, but Experience has since been consulted and
the answer is, touch not without personal merit;
on the other hand pay not a long price for animals
that are not well descended ; purchase not such as
are merely puffed up for exhibition purposes by a
mass of fat, but buy in a natural state and keep
them in a natural way—

> And breed only from tho best
> That will stand the blast from east and west.

Through the depressed times Fashion has still
held its position where personal merit has not been
absent, but where it has been united with Prejudice
and depending entirely upon pedigree, it has fallen to
an extremely low ebb, from where it will not rise
without the aid of Prudence by judicious breeding,
in having not only good blood but personal
excellences blended together which is the only sure
way to a successful issue either iu old tribes or
the newly founded families. The writer knows that
in the eyes of many his ideas are travelling upon
forbidden ground, yet feels that his Experiences
will not be complete without making a few remarks
upon the tribes that Mr. Bates left us. Have the
Duchesses retained their former celebrity by their
breeders adhering strictly to Duchess or Oxford

z

blood? Have they not been frequently on the very
brink of falling over the dreaded precipice by
clinging to Fashion and Prejudice? But have not
some of their owners seen their dangerous position
and wisely adopted a safer course to preserve their
purity? Are the Oxfords a better class of animal
by being constantly allied with the Duchesses than
they were when Mr. Bates left them? Do the
Barringtons possess the same grandeur as they did
after the immediate alliance with Grand Turk and
Grand Duke 3rd by the continuation of Dukes,
Grand Dukes, or Oxfords? I can safely answer no,
except where the introduction of Marmaduke 14897,
was brought in through the blood of Duke of
Brailes; here we have not only personal merit and
purity blended together, but preserved. May I not
ask do the Lady Bates branch of this popular
family continue to improve by their long continuation of strictly pure crosses after the despised
addition of Mr. Harvey Coombe's The Buck? I am
afraid not. Are the descendants of Wild Eyes 23rd
better than she was herself? They were good cattle
when they left Mr. Maynard's, also when they left
Winterfold, but the all-important question is, are
they as good to day? Do they possess the same
amount of individual merit as they did before the
long continuation of in-bred sires? If not, why be
so slow to make a change in the system of
breeding? Deterioration in the animal deteriorates

the prices equally as much if not more than the depressed times. Neither can it be expected however superior they may be in merit to realize what they did in the palmy days of ten years back. A certain per centage must be allowed for the difference in business between 1887 and 1877, also an equal per centage in the difference between pedigree breeding and shorthorn breeding, as the prices of the former were entirely guided by the printing machine, the latter by purity of blood and personal merit blended together.

I have noticed during recent years many herds that are entirely built up from dairy cows, and now eligible for the Herd Book. Many males are sent from them to Bingley Hall for dispersion, and others are purchased for abroad. There are two reasons why this class of animals meet with a ready sale. Firstly, the price is not high, but still remunerative to the breeder; secondly, they are well grown for their age, generally good colours (the whites being steered) full of hair and taking to the eye. Being sent from the shorthorn herds of England is enough for many breeders in our distant lands. Perhaps I may not be out of place by giving a third reason why this class of animals are often more pleasing in appearance. Their breeders are generally practical men, often attending, and most frequently

superintending their own cattle and noticing their
small ailments in due time, which prevents the
veterinary being called in, or a disease from laying
hold of a vital part, and even more, the defective
points in the sire used in the latest generation is
avoided in the present one, as well as the weakest
constitutioned and ill-framed females being despatched to the shambles in their youth. On the
other hand fashionable herds are too often gathered
together wholesale, regardless of expense and
personal merit. All the bull calves they produce
must of course be reared for sires, no matter how
bad a colour or how mean looking he may be, he is
highly bred and his dam was a costly purchase from
Lord ———, and his sire was bred by the Duke of
———. If such breeding won't do, I don't know
what will! has frequently been the remark to the
writer from inexperienced breeders, and especially
from inexperienced agents, who have been diverted
from a gardener or a coolmaster, to be the
manager of a farm or small estate. The owner or
occupier of such a holding has frequently been
tempted into shorthorn breeding as a hobby, and sometimes under the idea of gaining a large percentage; so
the manager is sent to purchase a shorthorn or two at
the first sale that takes place; the agent returns
and informs his employer that he has bought the
best heifer in the sale, one that gained the prize
at the exhibition last year; of course she was

the fattest animal sold and a beautiful roan too; but
neither the agent nor his employer understood any
more how the animal was bred than she did herself.
How can such a course of breeding succeed or pros-
per? It requires the practical eye of experience
not only to purchase but to know how to breed, and
cultivate their produce from calfhood to avoid
delicacy in the following generation, as a sound
constitution is the first point to be considered in
laying the foundation of a herd of any description.
If the purchaser be possessed of ample means, lay
hold of well tried sorts for generations, as their
offspring by prudent cultivation are more reliable
than some of the new founded tribes that are now
eligible as shorthorns for the only reason that they
have a sufficient number of registered crosses.
Such a herd I observed only a few weeks ago that
had been bred for thirty-six years, from cattle
purchased in Darlington Market. Not many days
intervened before I had the opportunity of
inspecting another herd, bred in a similar manner
from animals selected about twenty-five years ago;
but by a different style of owner, although both were
tenant farmers, the former boasted of what his
animals were thirty-six years back; the latter put
before me the results of twenty-five years practical
work in a herd of a good sort and of one type, the
females prepared for the dairy and the males for the
market. The former had no shorthorn type of any

description, neither any special signs for the dairy,
nor immediate profit for the market. I admired
the extensive pastures they were grazing upon, but
could not, on turning away, be prevented saying—
Alas! the poor shorthorn has to take the blame for
it all! I travelled on for some miles distance
where I found an extensive herd, either purchased
by chance or which had been under the supervision of
the same master; here there were many useful cattle,
but of every sort imaginable. The owner of this
extensive herd was a thoroughly practical farmer
with the exception of this one point, and a very
important one in the eyes of the writer, as the
breeding of good live stock is the key to prosperity
in agriculture. Sires had been used for no other
reason than that they were bred by such a person, and
not that they were possessed of individual merit or
suitable for the females gathered together, consequently many of the dams were condemned unjustly
as bad breeders. Another day brings me a little
further north, where my eyes are intently fixed upon
a different class of cattle, yet of one style, still
different families; they are short-legged, well-
fleshed dairy cattle, and their produce showing a
similarity to themselves they have been bred carefully for the last twenty years upon the same farm,
and from old families even then. I also observed
new ones that were springing up, some of which
will at a future day make their mark in shorthorn

history.   Because an animal has the sufficient
number of registered crosses it does not always
become entitled to have the shorthorn character, as
character or type is important for the production of
good animals, and to procure them, the writer
would say, begin with that type even if it be only
from a dairy cow; he has himself had animals
become eligible by the required number of crosses
that were never fit to be classed as shorthorns.
The backs of the original cow, its daughters and
grand-daughters, were more like a fish set upon
edge than a shorthorn; others that he possessed
were from a grand beast with one registered cross,
that had the true character of a shorthorn, but
there was something beyond that assisted him to
produce the good animals, it was the work of others
before, and not his own.   Are there not such
animals even to day that are worthy of selection by
small capitalists or new beginners?   Many would
say with the writer that it is safer—

> For small boats to sail near shore,
> To cling to dairy shorthorns and nothing more.

CHAPTER XII.

THINGS AS THEY WERE, THE STORY OF THREE
COMPANIONS, THE THREE DRAWINGS, EXPERIENCES
INTERMIXED, THINGS AS THEY ARE, CONCLUDING
REMARKS.

The writer must not forget the promise that he
has previously made not to allow his readers to fall
asleep; to carry this out practically there is no
other course open for him but to intermix his
experiences in the concluding chapter, that it may
enable him to oblige all who kindly offered their
advice as to the contents of this work that he is
now about completing. To arrive at this clearly he
thinks it better for his thoughts to wander back
once more to the days of youth, when it was
scarcely thought respectable to attend either church
or chapel without being adorned in a long crowned
hat and swallow-tailed coat; it was in these days
that he, remembers seeing the parson (as he was
then called) milking his own cow and repairing his
own hedge ; his church, or probably known better by
the name of a chapel, was divided more like a
a building for cattle than a place of Divine worship;
such as. could afford, or had an interest in their
church had their portions partitioned off, while
others allowed their seats to be divided by a single

rail and to remain an eartheru floor to be bestrewed over with bent from the banks of the river Duddon. It is also still fresh in his memory seeing the choir master stand up alone—how interesting such a sight would be in the year 1887!

Can any be surprised if the history that is written should prove to be a little old fashioned, when I say that style then was scarcely known, and fashion, as it is known now, almost a stranger, but evidently Prejudice was a frequent visitor, or more probably took up his abode there, as I often observed that every building for farm purposes was built upon one plan, with the exception of my father's, which he had recently erected on a more elaborate scale. The rest of the property in the township was divided into fourteen estates, and singular to say each estate had one cattle shed that provided room for twelve animals in every instance but two, which had provision for sixteen, but all were built upon the same principle, with stabling for four horses, and a large barn for hay and corn (in preference to ricks being made), attached to the other building, there not being such a thing as the ordinary one with the open yard, as we have them in the Midland Counties, or in the south of England; the winters there were considered too severe to allow cattle the privilege of the open air, but were confined in the building with the principal

AA

ventilation stopped, aud sometimes even the finger
hole for the latch carefully patched up with straw,
for fear the delicate animal should catch cold after
giving birth to a calf, or milking heavily.   These
were the ideas of my ancestors, and of the people
around my native home, how to treat the dumb
animals, which arc now termed shorthorns.   In the
spring they were released from the gloomy cell, but
had to go forth into the open air in their prison
garments, as they had been stripped of their winter
coats by close confinement, which prevented nature's
assistance in the growth of their natural protection
from wind and storm, that frequently resulted by
having to call in the veterinary, when the usual
spring verdict was given in the following words :—
" Caught cold, a chill from exposure. she is rather
delicate, give her a little bran followed by these
powders, and keep her warm until I call again."—
Another visit was made when a second release is
granted, and the poor beast once more in the open
air, but this time clothed in a thick coat, ordered
by the attendant, to prevent her again taking cold.
Prejudice or want of experience had not allowed
nature to provide the poor animal with hair that
was most natural for health and protection against
the surgeon's figures.   When the vine and the fig-
tree could stand the bitter blasts of winter and bear
fruit the following season, surely the dumb animals
ought not to have required more than ordinary

shelter. My father being a little ahead in the improvement and management of live stock, he informed them he had given £30 for one beast ; the villagers exclaimed if he was not mad then,he soon would be, as there was no such thing as one animal being worth that sum of money. This was the opinion of the agriculturalists known in the days of my childhood, which left an impression that made me often wonder and anxious to know who was right, but have since found that it was only by experience that I could have my anxiety relieved. But even then there were various degrees of opinion and especially upon agricultural matters. When Farmer Joe had to place a son upon a farm, he said he found it could not be done liberally for less than £100, as it would take fully £20 to furnish a house respectable in appearance for the young man to bring his bride, and to stock the land sufficiently could not be accomplished for less than £80! How this made the old farmer sigh, another £100 gone and still seven sons and four daughters to give a start in life. He stood aghast with his eyes and ears wide open when he heard that the Squire's son was about to furnish a house that would cost as much to complete one room as the whole of his son's house and farm had done ; could such things really be? was the old man's inquiry. Yes! was the reply, but what was fashionable then to Farmer Joe was not to the Squire's son, and what was fashionable

to the latter was useless to the former, and as there
was then to a certain extent different degrees in
fashion so there are still, but to arrive at my
meaning more clearly I shall pass on to speak of
another generation, as I well remember three boys
that were all born within twenty miles of each
other, whom I shall call by the names of Tom, Jim,
and Harry.   They were companions in their early
life, but widely different in disposition which
divided their opinions, and caused each youth to
choose a separate companion.   Harry, always bright,
cheerful, and generous, was a general favourite; he
selected a gay young fellow known by the name of
Fashion as his intimate friend and counsellor, who
led him on at a rapid rate, but Harry himself, who was
anxious to make his mark in the world, was not
behind in perseverance; but sad to say, it was all
done by the aid of his friend.   He commenced in
life, determined to succeed, as a farmer, but in one
branch more especially he was anxious not to be left
behind, and that was as a shorthorn breeder.   He
began to build up a herd to his own taste, but soon
found that for want of experience it was contrary to
the   ideas   of   Fashion,   so   it   was   repeatedly
built up and thrown down, to rebuild again, as
he was ambitious to have the best of blood, at any
cost.   Harry was undoubtedly clever at his business,
and could almost do as he wished in his prosperous
days. He was looked upon by the Nobility as one of

the most far-seeing and popular shorthorn breeders
in his own county, but being still more ambitious
ventured at last a little too far, by attempting to
cross the rapids ; but his boat was too slightly
built to withstand the strong current, and was
carried down the river by the stream of Fashion,
but fortunately rescued at the last by the strong
arm of Experience.

Harry's cousin Jim was not so attractive a youth
as himself, so had to be content with a companion
naturally not so refined, whose name was Prejudice.
Poor Jim had the good fortune not to be carried
away by the stream of Fashion, but was sorely
beaten upon the rocks by his friend Prejudice,
before his eyes were opened by Experience; he
too like his cousin was fond of shorthorns, and
determined to have the best, but in as much
a different way as there were in their characters; he
had no desire to build up and throw down, and
rebuild again as Harry had done, but when he had
once attained the honour of having a good herd, he
imagined his work was done, as his friend Prejudice
had great influence over him by persuasion that
there were few herds equal to his own, and that it
required no improvement, but it was rather the
judgement of his fellow breeders that was deficient.
If he exhibited his cattle without success, the poor
judges that distributed the prizes had to be con-

demned for their wrongful distribution.   Many
years have since then passed away, when an
aged friend, known by the name of Experience,
called by the way, and bid Prejudice to make a
hasty retreat, as the owner of the herd had at last
become awake and seen that there were other good
herds besides his own, as well as good breeders.

But I must not take up my readers' time any
longer respecting Jim and Harry, neither must I
omit naming the experiences of their friend Tom
as a breeder of shorthorns.   As a youth he was
naturally slow, and would not be led by Fashion,
nor held by Prejudice, but selected " Prudence " as
his friend to assist him to persevere in building up
a herd of useful shorthorns ; he soon found that
breeding to please the public was no easy duty to
perform, and that it could not be accomplished
without time and experience, so he gradually began
to build up a herd that would be known by its usefulness in the locality where it was bred ; he did
not venture to cross the rapids by Fashion, neither
did he allow himself to be beaten upon the rocks
in being bound to Prejudice, but built up his herd
year by year, and step by step, until he had accomplished his object in breeding cattle that would be
acceptable both to his pocket and the public.   He
did not make use of Prejudice as a weapon against
Fashion, neither was he bound as a slave to either,

as the two cousins were before they had been taught their bitter lessons by experience. Each young breeder persevered to have the best of herds, but in very different ways,—Harry depending on Fashion alone, Jim prejudiced against Fashion, by thinking he could do without it, Tom not only persevered but annexed Fashion and Prudence to satisfy the demands of the market, both in pedigree and personal appearance, while his two friends, one of which neglected the pedigree by Prejudice, and the other the appearance of the animal by Fashion.

Have we not breeders in the present generation that might be known by the names of Tom, Jim, and Harry, that are prejudiced either for or against fashion, or for their own herds and against others, imagining they have the best of animals and the best of blood, and who are not convinced to the contrary until they have been taught from the book of Experience. The most valuable lessons that the writer has ever been taught was in seeing the deficiency in his own herd by comparing it to those that were superior, that had gradually been built up step by step by men of judgement. Surely I have dwelt sufficiently upon my experiences as well as upon breeders of the past and present. I have spoken of the former from the days of Messrs. Collings up to the year 1880. Respecting what has taken place since that date, I have made but few

observations, either upon shorthorns or breeders,
for fear the contents of my work should clash with
the history of " The Shorthorn Herds of England,"
which has recently made its appearance from the
publisher's hands; it contains far more general
information upon shorthorns than anything I have
explained upon these few pages, that are simply
written from the experiences gained either by
practical observations upon the doings of others, or
what the writer has actually had the privilege of
doing himself up to middle life.   The expressions
used in composition are not borrowed from another,
neither are they the words of some learned man,
written in a fluent language of things that he has
seen in different countries, but they are simply
words compiled by one who has not had the
privilege of learning different languages or seeing
different countries, but has had to be content with
the education of the village school, beyond what
that great master, Experience, has taught him
since he left it.

   " What a peculiar picture to place in the centre
of a book upon shorthorns !" will, I have no doubt,
be the exclamation from many a reader at the first
sight of the largest drawing that it contains; therefore it is necessary for a few remarks to be made upon
them all by the author who designed them, before
bringing his history to a close.   The first that is
placed upon the title page simply contains Exper-

ience (the elder) and his four pupils as named in the introductory chapter; it is unnecessary to point them out individually as the skilful hand of the artist has well defined the expression of their countenances. The companion picture on the opposite page represents five different classes of animals as they are bred by their different style of breeders. The centre piece is a pure bred shorthorn, having a combination of the blood of such animals as the experienced, persevering and fashionable breeder would prudently permit. Figure 2, Prudence, her daughter, winner at the Dairy show, is both profitable and highly descended, but passes into the hands of the persevering youth who breeds from her Figure 3, an animal with a table back, and a winner at the Royal, but a loser at the pail in herself and her produce. The owner and breeder of Figure 4 through being prejudiced for years against the blood from the man of experience, has lost substance, constitution and beauty. Figure 5, daughter of Figure 3 is so extremely fashionably bred that her owner deems it not desirable to destroy the purity of her pedigree by admitting the blood admired by Mr. Prudence, therefore the superiority of the animal and pedigree is sacrificed at the shrine of fashion at Smithfield.

The third is an allegory upon every day life, the ten characters it represents are already introduced in the Second Chapter of Part II. According to

BB

the ideas of the designer this drawing has a three-fold meaning, but he does not feel himself bound to give any explanation further than what is relating to shorthorn breeding. Figure 1, Experience (the younger), represents a man gaining knowledge as a breeder by observing the doings of the different characters around him. 2, Spendall, is intended for extreme Fashion in everything, either as a purchaser, breeder or feeder, and even in pedigree. 3, Prejudice, by his countenance has evidently set his face not only against himself, but tries to prevent others being successful in their career. 4, Perseverance, continually climbing onwards and upwards by the aid of Figure 5 his friend Prudence. 6, Thrift, or Enterprise of 1886, one who has risen to his fashionable and profitable position by persevering to avoid prejudice, through prudence and experience. 7, Grumbler, discontented with his success as a breeder, and all others that have surpassed him. 8, Saveall, a perfect miser in all things, not fitted to breed or rear any kind of stock, as through his niggardliness the true shorthorn type would be destroyed. 9, Thrift, or Enterprise of 1846, clever in his day, but too old fashioned to compete with Enterprise of 1886. 10, Whitewash, one who loves self-praise, and promises great things; he perseveres to be a successful breeder, through his friends Saveall, Spendall, Grumbler, and the man out of fashion, by attempting to travel over the mountain of Ambition to reach the rich valley of Position, but prevented by Experience and Enterprise.

Who could have foretold not more than a couple of years ago that a resident in the old Manor House would so soon not only become a contributor to the press, but a designer for the artist of what he has either done or seen on his journey in life? But who can wonder that his experiences are not the most fashionable when he is dwelling in the midst of so many pieces of ancient workmanship? What building looks more stately than Warwick Castle? How can the writer's mind dwell continually upon shorthorns when he is surrounded by history? Have we not Stoneleigh Abbey, with its beautiful grounds, within a pleasant walk from the old Castle, and is not there the town of Warwick close at hand, admired by lovers of nature for its ancient buildings and picturesque scenery? Have we not Kenilworth Castle surrounded by its warlike ruins within an easy drive from where the author is drawing his conclusive remarks? Are we not in the midst of other places of interest? Does not the river Avon—with its graceful willows— flow silently along close to the dwelling of Shakespeare, where visitors are daily going to and fro, charmed with the idea that they have cast their eyes upon the spot where the great poet once resided? Can any one be surprised that I muse for a time on the works of art achieved by our ancestors?   But my attention must next be given to the Manor House which is not void of interest, in the memory of ancient people who lived there in years gone by, who prized the carved mantle-piece and the old-fashioned grate, who also erected a stone in full view from the window in remembrance of their faithful dog, but the writer's eye is fixed upon something more interesting beyond the iron paling than the remembrance of the past.   What can the object be he is so intently gazing upon?   It is not the grand architecture of the old castles, neither is it the ancient dwelling of Shakespeare, nor even the peaceful river gliding swiftly along, but it is nothing less than a group of shorthorns grazing in the Park. What scene could be more attractive or what picture more beautiful to a writer upon shorthorns. Is it not a work of art and industry that can give both pleasure and profit provided it is painted in its true colours by the hand of Experience.

The writer must not omit naming that his residence is within a day's march from the town of Fashion, where the occupiers are busily intent upon enjoyment, driving here and there in search of nature's charms amidst the aristocratic seats by which their houses are thickly surrounded, as well as the magnificent Town Hall, the Baths, the

Springs, and the Garden of Pleasure. Not many miles distant stands the town of Prejudice, once so famed for its visitors, but now superseded by the town of Fashion, but many of the inhabitants are still blind enough not to see that they are left behind the times by dependence upon what their town was, fifty years back, and not what she is in the year 1887.

Is there not a lesson to be learned from the two towns, one of which was both fashionable and business-like a century ago, but the other is so to-day. Are there not old breeders that can be compared to the former, who are still thinking that their herds are the best owing to their superiority in times past, but in reality are now surpassed by herds of the present fashion. Although the writer is deeply in love with old tribes it does not signify that they are always the best animals because they descend from aristocratic parents, or from the herds of enterprising men in years gone by, but which of the old families are the best to day is the question to ask ourselves. Have not many of them deteriorated as animals through the fashion of in-breeding and their owner being against the desirable tincture of new blood; such families have fallen in prices, others have been carelessly bred for generations without Fashion, Prejudice or inbreeding; they too have been reduced in value and I am afraid

as animals are not superior to what they were before
the obnoxious admixture was added; yet there are
many that have been carefully crossed for ages,
without that persistency of the idea that my
breeding is superior to thine, and where the owner's
head has not been lifted too high to see a good
animal behind his neighbour's hedge. To such
old tribes the writer would say, cling closely, but
Experience adds not by either excessive Fashion or
Prejudice, but through Perseverance by prudent
selection of sires. Certainly we have passed
through a number of years of depression, or, as
some may term it, depreciation in the value of
shorthorns, yet a true-made, robust-constitutioned,
and highly descended animal will always command
a ready customer at a paying price; but some may
ask how are this class of animals to be produced?
First of all it is desirable to have a genial climate,
sheltered against storm and heat, a suitable soil,
with a regular supply of water, and preferable if it
should pass through the farm by a running stream.
This is a sufficient foundation to begin to build
upon, but as I have already spoken at some length
respecting both the foundation and material, I must
not conclude without another word in connection
with the builder by asking a question. Did ever
an inexperienced builder commence to build a
Palace? If he unwisely did so, was it ever completed satisfactorily by his own hand? There is

but one answer that can be given either for him or any other inexperienced man of business or profession. How then is it possible for an extensive herd of shorthorns even with a good foundation laid, and costly material, to be built up by an inexperienced owner. Such an important work can only be accomplished step by step, as the builder adds stone to stone to reach the utmost extremity in the completion of a tower. In like manner the successful shorthorn breeder begins to build up his herd from the foundation, studying day by day, and year by year the best course to pursue until he has accomplished his work of art, wrought out only by time and experience.

The author of "Shorthorn Experiences" does not lay down his pen without knowing that his remarks are not the most fashionably expressed, but he trusts they are practicable, and free from prejudice. He has endeavoured by perseverance to bring out his book upon his experiences in as interesting and instructive a manner as possible, but leaves it entirely in the hands of his readers to decide whether his remarks are made with prudence.

> Perseverance moves onward up the hill,
> Prudence assists with all good-will,
> Fashion boasts he holds the sway,
> Experience steps in and says him nay,
> But Prejudice still remains behind,
> Years have roll'd on since he left my mind.

www.ingramcontent.com/pod-product-compliance
Lightning Source LLC
Chambersburg PA
CBHW030327270326
41926CB00010B/1534